SARTRE: A GUIDE FOR
THE PERPLEXED

Guides for the Perplexed available from Continuum:

Adorno: A Guide for the Perplexed, Alex Thomson

Deleuze: A Guide for the Perplexed, Claire Colebrook

Levinas: A Guide for the Perplexed, B. C. Hutchens

Sartre: A Guide for the Perplexed, Gary Cox

Wittgenstein: A Guide for the Perplexed, Mark Addis

SARTRE: A GUIDE FOR THE PERPLEXED

GARY COX

continuum
LONDON • NEW YORK

CONTINUUM
The Tower Building   15 East 26th Street
11 York Road   New York
London SE1 7NX   NY 10010

First published 2006
www.continuumbooks.com

© Gary Cox 2006

British Library Cataloguing-in-Publication Data
A catalogue record for this book is available from the British Library.

ISBN: HB: 0-8264-8705-X
PB: 0-8264-8706-8

Library of Congress Cataloging-in-Publication Data
A catalog record for this book is available from the Library of Congress.

Typeset by Servis Filmsetting Ltd, Manchester
Printed and bound in Great Britain by
MPG Books Ltd, Cornwall

For Sharon

CONTENTS

List of Abbreviations   viii
Preface   xi

Part 1 Consciousness   1
  1 Being-for-Itself   3
  2 Being-for-Others   42
  3 The Body   49

Part 2 Freedom   59
  4 Existential Freedom   61

Part 3 Bad Faith   89
  5 The Phenomenon of Bad Faith   91
  6 The Faith of Bad Faith – The Primitive Project   123

Part 4 Authenticity   131
  7 Sartre on Authenticity   133
  8 Sartre and Nietzsche   146
  9 Sartre and Heidegger   151

Notes   157
References   169
Further Reading   173
Index   174

LIST OF ABBREVIATIONS

Works by Sartre are cited using the following abbreviations.
See References for full bibliographical information.

AJ	*Anti Semite and Jew*
AR	*The Age of Reason*
BN	*Being and Nothingness*
CL	*The Childhood of a Leader*
CP	*Crime Passionnel*
EAH	*Existentialism and Humanism*
LC	*Lettres au Castor*
N	*Nausea*
NE	*No Exit*
POM	*The Problem of Method*
SG	*Saint Genet*
TE	*The Transcendence of the Ego*
W	*Words*
WD	*War Diaries*

All things which exist, exist either in themselves or in something else.
(Benedictus de Spinoza, *Ethics*, First Part, Axiom I)

PREFACE

There are many popular accounts of Sartre's existentialism that tell of his radical and apparently peculiar opinions without really explaining why he held them. This book is for anyone who wants to dig deeper and gain an understanding of Sartre as a genuine philosopher rather than as a cult figure. It is certainly a book written for those studying Sartre in college or university who want to fathom the complexities of Sartre's major work, *Being and Nothingness*, but it is also a book written for the growing number of people who consider philosophy a source of personal enlightenment worthy of independent exploration. My guiding principle in writing this book has been to make Sartre's sometimes complex thought accessible to any reasonably serious reader without oversimplifying it in the process.

This book explores and critically assesses Sartre's central themes of consciousness, freedom, bad faith and authenticity. It also shows how these four central themes of Sartre's thought are intimately interconnected. The structure of this book is dictated by the fact that Sartre's view of authenticity makes sense only in light of his view of bad faith, his view of bad faith only in light of his view of freedom and his view of freedom only in light of his view of consciousness. The structure of this book has to be as it is.

Part 1 begins by developing an account of the relationship between being and non-being (nothingness) that forms the crux of Sartre's entire thought. This account exposes the ontological bones of his philosophy of mind, explains the dialectical nature of his logic and introduces much of his special terminology. In turn, these preliminaries facilitate a description and evaluation of his phenomenological theory of consciousness. It is argued that Sartre's philosophy of mind, characterized by his defence of intentionality and his attack on the notion of sensations, exposes a number of serious faults inherent in certain alternative viewpoints. This is not to say, however, that Sartre's theory of consciousness is without faults of its own. A number of difficulties are identified, such as his dismissiveness when it comes to considering the emergence of consciousness from being and his inconsistent mixture of realist and transcendental idealist elements. Part 1 moves on to explore Sartre's views on consciousness and temporality, self-consciousness, a person's consciousness of others and their consciousness of him and, finally, the relationship between consciousness and the body. As well as being of intrinsic interest to students of Sartre, these investigations into further aspects of his theory of consciousness introduce various notions vital to the comprehension of the subject matter of the three subsequent parts. It would, for example, be impossible to make proper sense of the way in which one mode of bad faith distorts the relationship between consciousness and the body without first understanding the relationship in its undistorted form.

In Part 2, I argue that Sartre's theory of freedom emerges out of a general dissatisfaction with the traditional debate between determinists and the proponents of free will. The traditional proponents of free will, though replete with refutations of hard determinism, largely fail to offer any positive account of freedom. Sartre, for his part, is held to be innocent of this charge, in that his existential phenomenology attempts not only to make room for freedom, but also to detail the ontological structures that comprise the phenomenon. These ontological structures are explored and, although it is held that Sartre's position is largely cogent, various criticisms are made. For instance, it is argued that Sartre's radical freedom thesis is too extreme to make complete sense, and that he mystifies choice by rendering it groundless. Various solutions to these problems are considered, such as those proposed by his fellow existentialist Merleau-Ponty.

Part 3 considers bad faith – a phenomenon that perhaps more than any other is peculiarly Sartrean. The account of bad faith that this book provides develops directly out of the account of freedom provided in Part 2. It is argued that bad faith is a peculiar possibility of freedom in so far as it involves choosing not to choose. Attention is also given to the common error that bad faith is equivalent to self-deception. It is argued that the traditional contradictory notion of self-deception should be superseded by the far more coherent notion of bad faith. The view that bad faith is a coherent notion is advanced through an exploration of its several modes as they are represented by Sartre's concrete examples of people in bad faith. In order to draw together Sartre's various thoughts regarding bad faith, the faith of bad faith is explored, a phenomenon that, in Sartre's view, underpins all particular projects of bad faith and makes them possible.

Part 4 investigates the elusive phenomenon of authenticity: the antithesis of bad faith in so far as bad faith is synonymous with inauthenticity. Here Sartre's own view of authenticity as the affirmation of freedom is illuminated by comparing it with the respective views of Nietzsche and Heidegger.

PART 1

CONSCIOUSNESS

CHAPTER 1

BEING-FOR-ITSELF

The being by which Nothingness comes to the world must be its own Nothingness.

(*BN*, p. 23)

BEING AND NON-BEING

Sartre's philosophy is an intricate web of interconnections. The first task facing any serious commentator on Sartre is to enter the intricate web of his thought in a manner that avoids entangling the reader in confusions that are never again shaken off; the kind of confusions that fuel the widespread misconception that Sartre's thought is itself a largely confused tangle of ill-formed ideas. Admittedly, Sartre has an erratic way of developing an argument, not least because he strives at every turn to mention the diverse implications of his thought. Also, like any great thinker, many of the products of his fertile mind require clarification and development. By no means, however, is his thought confused or ill-formed. This book attempts to show that his thought, despite certain serious difficulties, is highly structured and largely coherent.

The best means of entering the complex web of Sartre's thought is to examine his views regarding the relationship between being and non-being (nothingness). This relationship, as the title of his major work, *Being and Nothingness* suggests, is central to his entire philosophy and underpins every aspect of it. It follows, therefore, that comprehending the logic of this relationship is the key to simplifying Sartre's complexities and to understanding his many paradoxical and seemingly peculiar formulations. To comprehend the logic of this relationship is to pick up the nearest thing to a guiding thread to be found in the maze of his system.

Examining the relationship between being and non-being makes explicit the status of negation as Sartre conceives it. Making Sartre's view of negation explicit is vital to the larger aim of making explicit his view of consciousness, in so far as consciousness, as he conceives it, is fundamentally a non-being in relation to being that exists as a negation of being.

First, I want to compare Sartre's view of the relationship between being and non-being with the view of this relationship held by one of his major influences, Hegel. This comparison serves to elucidate certain features peculiar to Sartre's view of the relationship that a straightforward, non-comparative account fails to elucidate. As will be seen, Sartre holds that his account of the relationship between being and non-being is an improvement on the account of the relationship offered by Hegel.

Against the seemingly self-evident and common-sense view that being *is* and non-being *is not*, Hegel maintains in his *Science of Logic* the initially startling position that pure being and pure non-being are one and the same.[1] According to Hegel, pure being is indeterminate and immediate. By this he means that being is not related to itself or to anything other than itself. It is equal to itself and only to itself. It cannot realize this equality with itself, however, because it cannot reflect on itself as equal to itself. Reflection requires there to be a distinction between that which reflects and that which is reflected on. Pure being does not possess this characteristic or any characteristic of any kind. It has no determining features. It is without any determinants. As Hegel argues, it is wholly indeterminate. It does not even have the determinant of duration. Pure being is all at once. It is immediate. Furthermore, pure being has no regions with relations of identity or difference one with another. Pure being cannot be external to itself as parts of an object are external to other parts, because that would mean it contained otherness within itself. Pure being has no within opposed to a without; it is utter internality. Being, therefore, has no content. It is not, however, empty as an empty container is empty. It is pure emptiness. Hegel argues that pure being is pure indeterminateness and emptiness, without relation, externality or content. This description of pure being serves in every respect as a description of pure non-being, which Hegel describes as the absence of all determination and content; a complete emptiness equal with itself and undifferentiated in itself.

4

It is worth noting that the idea that pure being and pure non-being are the same did not originate with Hegel, even if he must be credited with giving it the detailed explanation it had long awaited. As Hegel himself points out, Heraclitus, the pre-Socratic philosopher, argued that '*being* as little *is*, as nothing *is*, or, all *flows*, which means all is *becoming*' (Hegel 1998, p. 83). The Heraclitian idea of becoming as the original unity and synthesis of being and non-being is the central focus of Hegel's ontology. For Hegel, ultimately and ontologically, there is neither being nor non-being, only becoming.[2]

In Hegel's view, being and non-being are pure abstractions of thought distinct only in thought. By abstracting, thought can arrest the flow of becoming and fix being and non-being in their opposition. This opposition derives directly from the abstract idea of the determinate being of being as opposed to the determinate nothingness of nothing. But, to repeat Hegel's claim, being and non-being considered separately are equally indeterminate. For Hegel, the non-abstract truth is that neither being nor non-being determines itself as such, but rather that each is determined by the other. In a sense, each is the other, but this is not a matter of an identity conceived on the basis of an abstract separation, but a matter of the immediate and perpetual vanishing of the one in the other.

For Hegel, then, pure being and pure non-being are the same. All is becoming by virtue of the fact that non-being depends upon and is determined by being, just as being depends upon and is determined by non-being.

Like Hegel, Sartre holds that non-being – as the negation of being – is ontologically dependent upon being. Unlike Hegel, however, he does not hold that being is ontologically dependent upon non-being. For Sartre, non-being simply discloses being and is not necessary to the being of being: 'we must understand not only that being has a logical precedence over nothingness but also that it is from being that nothingness derives concretely its efficacy. This is what we mean when we say that nothingness haunts being. That means that being has no need of nothingness in order to be' (*BN*, p. 16).

In Sartre's view there is no interdependence of being and non-being as Hegel thinks. Non-being, as the negation of being, is dependent upon being, but being is not dependent upon non-being, at least not ontologically. Epistemologically, being is dependent upon non-being in so far as it is only from the point of view of non-being that being is disclosed and differentiated.

In so far as being surpasses itself towards something else, it is not subject to the determinations of the understanding. But in so far as it surpasses itself – that is, in so far as it is in its very depths the origin of its own surpassing – being must on the contrary appear such as it is to the understanding which fixes it in its own determinations. (*BN*, p. 14)[3]

It can even be hypothesized that non-being arose in order that being be known; that being somehow undertook to give rise to non-being in order to cease being blind to itself. Sartre raises this hypothesis himself in his conclusion to *Being and Nothingness* only to dismiss it. I will appraise Sartre's dismissal of this hypothesis and his general position towards questions concerning the emergence of non-being in due course.

Hegel, according to Sartre, assumes that because all particular determinations of being involve negation – this is not that, here is not there, and so on – being as such is determined by negation. In Sartre's view, Hegel is wrong to treat being and nothing as logically contemporary and ontologically interdependent. He argues instead that as the negation of being, requiring being in order to be being-denied, non-being must be logically subsequent to being: 'logically, nothingness is subsequent to being since it is being first posited, then denied' (*BN*, p. 14). In other words, negation, as the determination of being in the form of particular nihilations of being, must be the internal negation of an indeterminate being that is logically prior to the negation. The logical priority of being over non-being means that being cannot be made to depend on non-being. What is prior cannot depend for its being upon what is subsequent. If, ontologically speaking, there can only be being and non-being, and being is logically prior to non-being, then being must be grounded upon itself, or, as Sartre prefers to say, being must be *in-itself*. 'Being *is*. Being is in-itself. Being is what it is' (*BN*, p. xlii). Hence, he names being *being-in-itself*, though he usually abbreviates this as *in-itself*, a convention I will follow where appropriate.

Sartre's argument for the logical priority of being over non-being justifies his claim that his view of the relationship between being and non-being is superior to Hegel's. Hegel cannot be correct in claiming that being and non-being are logically equivalent if non-being is the negation or denial of being. Emptiness must be emptiness of something. The following passage summarizes Sartre's position, as against Hegel's, regarding the ontological status of being and non-being:

> For if I refuse to allow being any determination or content, I am nevertheless forced to affirm at least that it *is*. Thus, let anyone deny being whatever he wishes, he can not cause it not to be, thanks to the very fact that he denies that it is this or that. Negation can not touch the nucleus of being of Being, which is absolute plenitude and entire positivity. By contrast Non-being is a negation which aims at this nucleus of absolute density. Non-being is denied at the heart of being. When Hegel writes, '(Being and nothingness) are empty abstractions, and the one is as empty as the other,' he forgets that emptiness is emptiness of something. Being is empty of all other determination than identity with itself, but non-being is empty of being. In a word, we must recall here against Hegel that being is and nothingness is not. (*BN*, p. 15)

I have opened my account of Sartre's ontology by comparing it with that of Hegel. I will now expand on Sartre's position, starting with *being-in-itself*. Although Sartre holds that the only thing that can be said about being-in-itself is that it is irrespective of non-being, he does attempt to elaborate on the pure isness of being-in-itself in various ways: 'It is a full positivity. It knows no otherness; it never posits itself [as its negation does] as *other-than-another-being*' (*BN*, p. xlii). As all else is logically subsequent to being-in-itself, it cannot be said of being-in-itself that it is derived from the possible. According to Sartre, the possible is a structure of that which is logically subsequent to being, namely, *being-for-itself*. Neither can being-in-itself be reduced to the necessary. If it was necessary, it would be determined as that which cannot not be, when in fact it is in itself utterly without determination. This is the contingency or superfluity of being-in-itself. 'Being is superfluous . . . consciousness absolutely can not derive being from anything, either from another being or from a possibility, or from a necessary law. Uncreated, without reason for being, without any connection with another being, being-in-itself is *de trop* for eternity' (*BN*, p. xlii).

All that can really be said about being-in-itself, as Sartre conceives it, is that it is. A much more detailed account can be given, however, of Sartre's view of non-being. Consciousness, as conceived by Sartre, is fundamentally and ontologically a non-being in relation to negation of being. Therefore, the following account of view of non-being is to be understood as an account of his the being of consciousness at the ontological level. My main aim at present is to make explicit Sartre's thoughts regarding the ontological foundation of consciousness. Flesh will be put on these ontological bones in due course when the account of Sartre's view of consciousness assumes a phenomenological focus.

Sartre's account of non-being is like this: being-in-itself, unlike non-being, is what it is and not what it is not. Nevertheless, what it is not (non-being) *is*. Not in the sense of being it – this would make non-being indistinguishable from being-in-itself – but in the sense of *having to be* it. Unlike being-in-itself, which simply *is* without having to achieve its being, non-being has to achieve, *for itself*, its being as the non-being of being-in-itself by perpetually negating being-in-itself. It has to be what it is *for itself* as the active negation of being-in-itself. Hence, Sartre names non-being *being-for-itself*, though he usually abbreviates this as *for-itself*.

If the for-itself was a passive emptiness of being it would be pure non-being, but it is not a passive emptiness alongside being; not a logically contemporary and independent being of emptiness. Such a being of emptiness would not be an emptiness of being, it would be a pure positivity. Like being, its emptiness would be an emptiness of determinations, not an emptiness of being. As such, it would be indistinguishable from being-in-itself. But to repeat: the for-itself is the negation of being. It is being first posited then denied. It is not the non-being of itself, it is the non-being of being. In not being the non-being of itself, the for-itself has to perpetually strive to be the non-being of itself without ever being able to become non-being-in-itself, or what Sartre calls *for-itself-in-itself*. Being-for-itself-in-itself, according to Sartre, is a perpetually desired but absolutely unrealizable state of being in which the negation of being becomes a negation-in-itself. 'It is the impossible synthesis of the for-itself and the in-itself' (*BN*, p. 90). In other words, it is an impossible state of being in which the nothingness that is the essence of being-for-itself exists with the full positivity of being-in-itself. It is widely held that God exists in this way. God is essentially a for-itself, a conscious, knowing being, yet his consciousness is held to exist fundamentally rather than as a relation or a negation. In short, God's existence and essence are assumed to be one. The Ontological Argument for the existence of God, first formulated by Anselm in his *Proslogion*, assumes this unity of existence and essence. For Anselm, the most perfect conceivable entity must have the attribute of existence. So, for Anselm, God's essence implies his existence. God is the ultimate for-itself-in-itself. This is why Sartre argues (*BN*, p. 566) that the fundamental, unrealizable project of the for-itself is to be God. As Richard Kamber writes: 'According to Sartre every desire (or motive) that a human being has is an expression of that person's fundamental choice of being (*what* that person desires to be), and every fundamental choice is an expression of our common human desire to be God!' (Kamber 2000, pp. 78–9). As Kamber also notes, and as will be seen in due course, Sartre's theory of bad faith makes much of the notion of people striving to be at one with what they are.

If the for-itself achieved identity with itself it would become being; it would collapse back into being. Therefore, the for-itself has both to be the perpetual project of negating being in order to realize itself as the negation of being, and the perpetual project of negating itself in order to refuse a coincidence with itself that would be its own annihilation. 'The for-itself is the being which determines itself to exist inasmuch as it can not coincide with itself' (*BN*, p. 78). In order not to collapse back into being – or, to be more precise, in order not to collapse into a pure non-being that left only being – the for-itself must be both an affirmation denied and a denial affirmed. The affirmation that is denied is being-in-itself; the denial that is affirmed is the for-itself's denial of itself as denial-in-itself; that is, the denial of itself as for-itself-in-itself. Unable to be a being determinate in-itself, either as being or as non-being, the for-itself has to be an ambiguous, indeterminate and paradoxical being. It has to be a perpetual double negation. Sartre describes the paradoxical nature of the for-itself in a series of formulations that are central to his entire theory:

> it is a being which is not what it is [being] and which is what it is not [nothing]. (*BN*, p. 79)

> human reality is constituted as a being which is what it is not and which is not what it is. (*BN*, p. 63)

> At present it is not what it is (past) and it is what it is not (future). (*BN*, p. 123)

The paradoxical nature of the for-itself is best understood in terms of temporality. This will be considered in due course.

As noted, being-for-itself expresses the being of consciousness at the fundamental or ontological level. When discussing being-for-itself, Sartre sometimes gives the impression that he is referring to a single metaphysical essence. The reason for this is perhaps, quite simply, his habit of referring to it as *the* for-itself, which tends to suggest a single, universal mode of being. This, however, is not his intention, and generally he is quite clear that being-for-itself is always and only the way of being of each individual embodied consciousness. In a sense, *being-for-itself* is merely a useful technical term referring to that which is common to any consciousness whatsoever, without implying thereby that there is anything beyond the series of particular consciousnesses. The following passage from Sartre concerning feudalism and the individual for-itself that happens to exist within the context of feudalism illustrates the point:

> Feudalism as a technical relation between man and man does not exist; it is only a pure abstract, sustained and surpassed by the thousands of individual projects of a particular man who is a liege in relation to his lord . . . In the same way the For-itself can not be a person – i.e., choose the ends which it is – without being a man or a woman, a member of a national collectivity, of a class, of family, etc. (*BN*, p. 523)

Nevertheless, Sartre insists that light is shed on these thousands of individual projects by considering them in terms of the technical relation of feudalism, just as light is shed on all individual life-projects by considering them in terms of the relationship between for-itself and in-itself.

A possible objection at this point is that such an overarching generalization about people stereotypes them and denies their diversity; that phenomenology is as open to the charge of reductionism as psychology, which does not so much explain people as explain them away by translating a personal understanding of them into the impersonal terms of it-processes.[4] Such a charge may well be pertinent when levelled against psychology. It is not pertinent, however, when levelled against phenomenology. Establishing that all people are, ontologically speaking, a for-itself in relation to the in-itself, far from denying diversity, reveals how the vast diversity of humankind is made possible. As will be seen, establishing that all people are, ontologically speaking, a for-itself in relation to the in-itself is the first step towards establishing that all people are free with no essence other than that which they perpetually choose and create.

I must now tackle an issue raised earlier: an issue set aside until my account of Sartre's view of being and non-being was more fully developed. It was noted that Sartre dismisses the hypothesis that being somehow undertook to give rise to the for-itself in order that it (being) be known. Sartre's objection to this hypothesis is that it attributes to being the capacity of having projects that only a for-itself can possess. Sartre holds that only a being that is what it is not can have projects, because only a being that is what it is not can aim to be other than it is. In so far as being is what it is, it could not have undertaken the project of giving rise to the for-itself. If Sartre's view that being-in-itself simply *is* accepted, then his view that the for-itself cannot be accounted for in terms of any kind of intention on the part of being-in-itself must also be accepted. Sartre, however, not only rejects this particular, and rather weak, attempt to account for the emergence of the for-itself, he rejects on principle all attempts to account for the emergence of the for-itself. In his conclusion to *Being and Nothingness* he argues that any attempt to account for what he describes as the upsurge of the for-itself from being produces only hypotheses that cannot possibly be validated or invalidated. As far as Sartre is concerned, the upsurge of the for-itself from being must be accepted as axiomatic, just as the being of being must be accepted as axiomatic. Sartre makes this claim with such an air of finality that it scarcely occurs to critics to challenge him. But must the upsurge of the for-itself simply be accepted as an unfathomable mystery? After all, the upsurge of the for-itself must have occurred somehow. At the very least, there must be better and worse conjectures, suggesting that conjecturing about the upsurge of the for-itself is more productive than Sartre allows.

In attempting to outline a reasonable starting-point for a theory of the emergence of being-for-itself it can be said that being-for-itself expresses, ontologically, the way of being of every conscious human organism (excluding, possibly, very young children); whereas it does not express the way of being of organisms lower down the evolutionary scale. This being so, it might be possible to develop an evolutionary theory of the emergence of being-for-itself which explains the development of consciousness and identifies the point at which fully developed consciousness as exemplified by (modern) humans was finally reached. Conjecture can begin in the following way about the major stages along the path from primitive, non-conscious life-forms to a life-form possessing fully developed consciousness. Successful environment-seeking required increased sensitivity – perception. Sophisticated environment-seeking required recollection of situations absent from present experience – thought. Communication of such recollections to other members of the species – basic language. Cooperation between members of the species to shape the environment, and regulation of relations between members of the species involved in this enterprise – highly evolved language, self-concept, conscience.

Given his generally dismissive attitude toward the natural world, Sartre would probably be hostile to this kind of naturalistic account.[5] Yet rejecting a naturalistic account of the emergence of consciousness – for which there is, after all, a wealth of scientific evidence – invites instead a metaphysical account that seeks to explain the emergence of consciousness as a magical and mysterious gift of the gods. Sartre the existentialist would surely dislike a metaphysical account of the emergence of consciousness even more than a naturalistic one.

I have considered the relationship between being and non-being: in Sartre's terms, the relationship between being-in-itself and being-for-itself. I have considered being-for-itself as that which expresses the being of consciousness at the ontological level. The next step is to consider Sartre's view of consciousness at the phenomenological level: consciousness as it is in its relation to the world.

SUBJECTIVITY AND OBJECTIVITY

As the negation of being, the for-itself is nothing in itself. It follows, therefore, that consciousness, as that which exists in the mode of being-for-itself, is also nothing in itself. Sartre acknowledges that 'This is what Hegel caught sight of when he wrote that "the mind is the negative"' (BN, p. 436).[6] He argues that as consciousness is nothing in itself its being must consist in its being consciousness of ___. 'Consciousness is consciousness of something . . . To say that consciousness is consciousness of something means that for consciousness there is no being outside of that precise obligation to be a revealing intuition of something' (BN, p. xxxvii). Consciousness does not first exist and then intend something; it exists only in so far as it intends something. The theory that consciousness exists only in so far as it posits that which it is consciousness *of* is known as intentionality. In his *Cartesian Meditations: An Introduction to Phenomenology*, Edmund Husserl, a major influence on Sartre, credits his own teacher, Franz Brentano, with discovering intentionality (Husserl 1977). In the following passage Brentano summarizes the theory of intentionality:

> Every mental phenomenon includes something as object within itself, although they do not all do so in the same way. In presentation something is presented, in judgement something is affirmed or denied, in love loved, in hate hated, in desire desired and so on. This intentional inexistence is characteristic exclusively of mental phenomena. No physical phenomena exhibit anything like it. We can, therefore, define mental phenomena by saying that they are those phenomena which contain an object intentionally within themselves. (*Brentano* 1973, pp. 88–9)

Investigating intentionality leads to a consideration of the intentional objects towards which consciousness is directed. Brentano, Husserl and Sartre agree that an intentional object is whatever consciousness is of or about, be it perceived, imagined, believed or felt emotionally. An intentional object is not a physical object. Phenomenologically, however, a physical object is an intentional object in the sense that a physical object is characterized phenomenologically as a collection of appearances and not as a physical thing. In the same way that a person's experience of a centaur is not of a physical thing but of an intentional object comprised of various appearances (literary references, artistic images, and so on), so his experience of a coin is the experience not of a physical thing but of an intentional object comprised of various appearances. Close up a coin appears large. If the coin is turned over different sides appear successively. Its shape appears differently as its orientation changes and its colour appears to alter with the light. The coin makes a sound as it hits the table. Far away the coin appears small. When reduced to its appearances in this way the physical or empirical object does not appear, but rather a succession of aspects. Responding to this a critic will argue that even though only particular aspects of the coin are experienced, these aspects indicate the coin-in-itself, the thing-in-itself (noumenon), as the ground or substratum of the aspects experienced. Phenomenologists reject this view. In their view, it involves the distinction between appearance and reality that the phenomeno-logical project seeks to overcome; the view that what is real is not what appears but a world behind the scenes that is forever hidden by a cloak of appearances. Phenomenology, instead of equating the physical object with a supposed ground or substratum, equates the physical object with all of its appearances, actual and possible. Appearances which are presently appearing do not indicate an underlying thing-in-itself, but rather further possible appearances that are not presently appearing but which could do so. In *Cartesian Meditations* Husserl calls these possible appearances *horizons*. Sartre calls them the *transphenomenal*.

In developing his view of transphenomenality Sartre argues that an examination of everyday experience reveals that the appearance of an object for consciousness is never the appearance of the whole object with all of its possible aspects at any one time, but rather the appearance of a particular aspect at a particular time. The appearance of a particular aspect is given as the experience of an object on the basis of the infinite series of possible appearances that do not appear. 'The appearance, which is finite, indicates itself in its finitude, but at the same time in order to be grasped as an appearance-of-that-which-appears, it requires that it be surpassed toward infinity' (*BN*, p. xxiii). All objects have hidden insides and other sides, a past that is no longer and a future that is not yet. Consciousness, as an absence itself, posits these absences by surpassing and transcending that which appears towards that which does not appear. That which appears is held to be the appearance of a real object if it has transphenomenal aspects. For Sartre, transphenomenality is the mark of the real. In his view, transphenomenality, the infinite series of possible appearances, must replace the old dualism of appearance and reality that has misled philosophers for centuries: 'the dualism of being and appearance is no longer entitled to any legal status within philosophy. The appearance refers to the total series of appearances and not to a hidden reality which would drain to itself all the being of the existent' (*BN*, p. xxi). There is, in Sartre's view, nothing beyond the appearance in the form of an absolute being that claims full pos-itivity while reducing the appearance to a mere shadow. If there is nothing beyond the appearance then full positivity is restored to the appearance, the essence of which 'is an "appearing" which is no longer opposed to being, but on the contrary is the measure of it' (*BN*, p. xxii).

It is at this point, just when it seems Sartre has solved the problem of appearance and reality, that a serious inconsistency arises in his thesis. On the one hand, judging by the kind of remarks quoted above, there is no doubt that Sartre is a realist about appearances. Appearances are not distinct from reality, they are reality. The appearance is a full positivity, the measure of being, and so on. Although phenomena appear to us, they exist as they appear to us independently of us. Yet, on the other hand, judging by other remarks that he makes, there is also no doubt that Sartre sees appearances as requiring a perceiving subject in order to have any reality as appearances. 'Relative the phenomenon remains, for "to appear" supposes in essence somebody to whom to appear' (*BN*, p. xxii). In this latter respect Sartre comes across not as a realist but as a form of transcendental idealist. He gives the clear impression of arguing for an undifferentiated being-in-itself which is differentiated into phenomena by the negations that consciousness places into being. In so far as this suggests that reality belongs to being-in-itself and not to phenomena that are only an appearance for consciousness, it does not seem to overcome the dualism of appearance and reality that Sartre aims to dismiss.

My answer to those trying to decide whether Sartre is a realist or a transcendental idealist is that he is, by turns, both! His thought exhibits these two incompatible positions not just slightly but to a significant extent. Questions as to which position is the more intelligible and which is the more deeply rooted in the structure of his thought can only be answered when fuller accounts of both Sartre the realist and Sartre the transcendental idealist have been given.

Sartre's realism. In his book *Using Sartre*, Gregory McCulloch develops an account of Sartrean direct realism by contrasting it with Cartesian indirect realism and Berkeleyan idealism or phenomenalism.

Cartesian indirect realists hold that the mind and the material world, though they interact somehow, are essentially independent of each other. As McCulloch points out (McCulloch 1994, p. 84): 'According to Cartesian realists both of the following are true:

1. The world could exist without any minds in it.
2. Minds could exist without any surrounding material world or environment.'

Cartesian realists hold that mind and world each have their own independent mode of existence. The mind is *res cogitans* – that which has ideas. The world is *res extensa* – that which is extended in space. If the mind is that which has ideas, it follows that it is directly aware of ideas rather than the world. Cartesian realists insist that ideas of the world, perceptions of the world, are caused by the world, but they have no real way of proving this and are unable to withstand the threat of solipsism.[7] If the mind encounters only ideas then how can it know that there is a material world external to the mind? Failure to resolve this issue encourages views that rule out the material world altogether.

In seeking to overcome the inherent difficulties of Cartesian indirect realism, Berkeleyan idealism denies the existence of a material world. It rejects claim (1) of Cartesian realism while retaining claim (2). Berkeleyan idealists reason that if the mind is not directly aware of material things then there are no grounds for claiming that material things exist. Material things must in fact be collections of ideas. These ideas have no mind-independent existence. They exist only in so far as they are perceived by a mind, a view encapsulated in the maxim, *esse est percipi* (to be is to be perceived). Berkeley's view implies that things cease to exist when they are not being perceived. His response to this is to argue that things do not cease to exist when we are not perceiving them because God perceives everything all the time. God's omnipresent awareness maintains the objectivity of the collections of ideas that form the world.[8]

The fact that claim (2) of Cartesian indirect realism is retained by Berkeleyan idealism reveals, despite their obvious differences, an important similarity in the respective positions of Descartes and Berkeley. Though they differ over what lies outside the mind, they share the view that the mind contains ideas as a gallery contains pictures. It is this picture-gallery model of the mind, shared by both Descartes and Berkeley, that Sartre challenges in arguing for direct realism. He wants to show that people are not aware of ideas, perceptions or visual representations of the world occurring inside the mind, but of the world itself. Sartre argues that the mind exists only in so far as it intends its object. Hence, he dismisses the notion of the mind as an independently existing realm of ideas in favour of his own radical approach to the two doctrines of Cartesian indirect realism. This approach, as McCulloch notes, involves a move contrary to that made by Berkeley. Berkeley rejects (1) and retains (2), whereas Sartre rejects (2) and retains (1). Unlike Descartes and Berkeley, Sartre does not view the mind as an in-itself that can exist without any surrounding material world or environment. Sartre, as seen, argues that consciousness is consciousness of __. As nothing in itself, consciousness must be consciousness of a surrounding world in order to be.

Sartrean direct realism avoids the following difficulties raised by Descartes' and Berkeley's picture-gallery model of the mind:

Exponents of the picture-gallery model often claim that the world we have knowledge of is not the one that we actually encounter. Taking visual experience as an example, they argue that all that is actually seen is a flat, coloured mosaic. This mosaic is transformed into the appearance of phenomena by certain processes in the mind or brain. Sartre objects to this mosaic theory not least because it seems absurd to him to suppose that the richness and complexity of visual experience is constructed out of mere patches of colour. We only have to look about. Do we see furniture, books, pens, paper, a world of character-laden, medium-size dry objects languishing around us, or do we see patches of colour? If we saw only patches of colour we would have to concentrate on forming these patches into a world of objects, but surely the reverse is true. What immediately strikes us, without any effort at all, is a world of intentional objects, and we have to concentrate very hard to get it to look anything like a flat mosaic. If we really only see patches of colour then why is it so difficult for us to see what we see? This argument wears away at the picture-gallery model, but it can still be objected that the most complex appearances are constructed out of the simplest elements. It can be argued, for example, that a TV image of Robert De Niro is really only a series of coloured dots, but this supposes that the coloured dots are the intentional object of awareness rather than De Niro. We can make the coloured dots rather than De Niro the intentional object of awareness by moving close to the screen, but from normal range we cannot even see the coloured dots as such. What we see is De Niro, the intentional object of the image. To claim that when we see De Niro on the screen what we really see is a series of coloured dots, is like claiming that we see a series of handsome, charismatic coloured dots striking curious poses, waging war, making love and smiling that De Niro smile. Surely the truth is that what we really see when we see a certain series of coloured dots is De Niro. If we deliberately make the coloured dots the object of awareness by moving close to the screen we lose sight of the image and no longer have any awareness of it.

The same kind of argument can be levelled against the claim that visual awareness is reducible to processes in the eyes and brain. Certainly, we cannot be aware of an image of De Niro without events taking place in the eyes and brain, but this does not mean that the image seen is only events in the eyes and brain. Seeing De Niro produces retinal response ABC and neurone-firing sequence XYZ, but these responses are not the image that is seen. Sartre argues that the eye-and-brain events that enable us to see the world are surpassed by consciousness. (This point will be explored further when I consider his view of the body.) There is no consciousness of the biological apparatus and events that enables us to be conscious of the world, any more than there is consciousness of the coloured dots that form a TV image when consciousness is of the TV image.

This inkwell on the table is given to me immediately in the form of a *thing*, and yet it is given to me by *sight*. This means that its presence is a visible presence and that I am conscious that it is present to me as visible – that is, I am conscious (of) seeing it. But at the same time that sight is *knowledge* of the inkwell, sight slips away from all knowledge; there is no knowledge of sight. My reflective consciousness will give to me indeed a knowledge of my reflected-on consciousness of the inkwell but not that of a sensory activity. (*BN*, pp. 315–16)

In criticizing the picture-gallery model of the mind, Sartre attacks the notion of sensations. The sensations theory, like the mosaic theory, holds that the world is a mental construct, but unlike the mosaic theory, which allows that there is some limited direct access to basic elements, the sensations theory denies that there is any direct access at all. The sensations theory holds that we are not directly aware of the world, but of impressions made on the sense organs. The crux of Sartre's argument against sensations is that the experience of white, for example, is not separable from the white experienced. Talk about the sensation of white posits a bastard existence distinct from a non-experienced white. The non-experienced white is assumed to give rise somehow to the sensation of white experienced. It is needless and mistaken, Sartre argues, to posit sensations as entities that both reveal and conceal the world at the same time. Sartre once took part in an experiment on vision. The psychologist conducting the experiment asked Sartre to describe his sensation of a yellow patch rather than the yellow patch Sartre was seeing. Sartre was struck by this, and later wrote:

> Sensation, a hybrid notion between the subjective and the object-
> ive, conceived from the standpoint of the object and applied sub-
> sequently to the subject, a bastard existence concerning which we
> can not say whether it exists in fact or in theory – sensation is a
> pure daydream of the psychologist. It must be deliberately
> rejected by any serious theory concerning the relations between
> consciousness and the world. (*BN*, p. 315)

Although it is possible to talk sensibly about bodily sensations, confusion arises when we start talking about sensory sensations. For example, it makes sense to say when having a snowball fight, 'I have a painful burning sensation in my hands', but it makes no real sense to say when looking at snow, 'I have a white sensation in my eyes.' A freezing object causes a sensation of pain, but a white object does not cause a sensation of white. The experience of white is not separable from the white object experienced as pain is separable from the freezing object that caused it.

To suppose that we see only coloured patches, or receive only visual sensations but are nonetheless aware of objects, is to suppose that the objects of our awareness are mental constructs; pictures in the mind seen by an inner observer. This view, which lies at the very heart of the picture-gallery model, is fraught with problems. For immaterialists there is the problem of how a picture, spatial by definition, can be contained within a mind that is not material. For materialists, there is the problem of how a coloured picture can appear in the darkness of the brain. Psychologists who declare that we see in darkness and hear in silence reveal themselves as exponents of the picture-gallery model.

The height of absurdity is reached with the notion of the inner observer, a notion that presents what is known as the homunculus problem. The absurdity of the notion lends itself to comedy – there is a sketch by Woody Allen and a comic strip, *The Numbskulls*, that present the brain as a control room peopled by technicians – yet something like this comical notion is widely endorsed. The problem is that if a person achieves awareness by virtue of an inner observer, then how does the inner observer achieve awareness? Does the first inner observer possess a second inner observer who possesses a third, and so on to infinity, or is the first inner observer directly aware of mental pictures in a way that the person is not directly aware of the world? If it can be argued that the first inner observer is directly aware then it would be less problematic to argue that the person is directly aware and do away with the homuncular inner observer. The problem of the inner observer is so serious that it is sufficient to warrant the complete abandonment of the picture-gallery model of the mind.

There is a view prevalent in cognitive science that seeks to hold on to the notion of homunculi while avoiding the problem of infinite regress. Cognitive science models consciousness as networks of inter-acting homunculi processing representations with each homunculus comprised of lower-order homunculi also processing representa-tions. This situation is supposed not to continue indefinitely but to bottom out with neurophysiological processors that do not deal in representations. Unfortunately, even though this notion avoids the problem of infinite regress, the claim that the regress bottoms out at the level of neurophysiology reintroduces a problem already con-sidered. It has already been argued that it makes no more sense to claim that consciousness of x is really only a physical event in the brain than it does to claim that a TV image is really only a series of coloured dots. Although consciousness cannot occur without phys-ical events in the brain occurring, consciousness is not reducible to physical events in the brain.[9] Consciousness is not physical events in the brain, but consciousness *of* something. Reducing consciousness to neurophysiological events in the brain and misrepresenting it in terms of a non-conscious in-itself excludes the possibility of inten-tionality, the defining feature of consciousness.

That appearances are not ideas in the mind does not imply that appearances are independent of the mind. Although in many places Sartre insists that appearances are independent of the mind, claim-ing that the world is as it appears even when it is not appearing to anyone, he offers no arguments that secure this claim. At most he appeals to common sense, insisting that the world must exist in all its diversity apart from anyone's awareness of it. Moreover, in many other places Sartre forsakes his claim that appearances are indepen-dent of the mind, endorsing, instead, transcendental idealism. That is, the view that appearances are dependent on the mind and must be appearances *to* __. To endorse this view is not to revert to claiming that appearances are ideas in the mind of a perceiver, but rather to hold that appearances appear out there, to consciousness, when consciousness arrives on the scene. As indicated earlier, Sartre's philosophy swings between realism and transcendental idealism, exhibiting a serious inconsistency that is seemingly impossible to play down or resolve.

Sartre's transcendental idealism. As a transcendental idealist Sartre holds that being-in-itself is undifferentiated. All that can be said of it is that it is: 'Being is. Being is in-itself. Being is what it is' (*BN*, p. xlii). Being is disclosed and differentiated only from the point of view of non-being; from the point of view of the for-itself. That is, it is only by virtue of the for-itself that being is transformed into phenomena or phenomenalized. Sartre undoubtedly draws a distinction between being-in-itself and phenomena. Some commentators have identified Sartre's distinction with Kant's 'two worlds' distinction between noumena and phenomena, in which a world of noumena is held to lie behind the world of phenomena. This is a traditional view of Kant – a view that has been subject to reappraisal by recent commentators who argue that Kant does not hold that noumena and phenomena denote two distinct realms of being. They argue that for Kant there is only a single realm of being that can be encountered from two distinct standpoints. Only a divine mind capable of non-sensible intuition can encounter being as noumena; as it is in itself. Ordinary minds capable only of sensible intuition must encounter being as phenomena.[10] This more recent and subtle interpretation of Kant is closer to what Sartre proposes. Sartre explicitly rejects the traditional view of Kantian noumena (*BN*, p. xxiv), arguing that being-in-itself does not lurk behind appearances as a noumenal foundation that underlies phenomena. For Sartre, because it is the negation of being that gives rise to phenomena, phenomena are founded not upon being, but upon non-being. Being is not the foundation of phenomena, being is the foundation of the non-being of the for-itself that phenomenalizes being by negating it. Recalling Sartre's view of the for-itself as a double negation helps clarify matters at this point.

The for-itself is the negation of being. Sartre calls this logically prior dimension of the double negation the radical negation. As the negation of being, however, the for-itself also negates being, not in the form of a radical negation of the very being of being, as Hegel supposes, but in the form of particular concrete negations of being. Sartre calls this dimension of the double negation the concrete negation. The radical negation is so called because it is the negation of the whole of being: 'The for-itself, which stands before being as its own totality, is itself the whole of the negation and hence is the negation of the whole' (*BN*, p. 181).

The concrete negation, on the other hand, is so called because it is that by which particular concrete phenomena appear – this as distinct from that, this as not that, this as external to that, and so on. Phenomena are for the for-itself, in the sense that indeterminate and undifferentiated being is determined and differentiated as distinct phenomena by the negations (the negativities or *négatités*) that the for-itself places into being. The negation negates in the form of particular negations of being.[11] In aiming at but not achieving the negation of being as a whole these particular negations realize phenomena as entities that are grounded not upon being but upon particular privations of being.

Particular privations of being arise when being is questioned. Sartre argues that our relationship to the world is primarily characterized by a questioning attitude. This questioning attitude is the constant pre-judicative expectation of a disclosure of non-being rather than the capacity to judge that something is lacking. 'If I question the carburettor, it is because I consider it possible that "there is nothing there" in the carburettor. Thus my question by its nature envelops a certain pre-judicative comprehension of non-being' (*BN*, p. 7).

Non-being arises whenever being is questioned, even if a reply is positive, even if there is something in the carburettor. This is not simply because the questioning attitude always raises the possibility of there being nothing there, the possibility of a negative reply, but because a positive reply entails negation as much as a negative reply. If it is the case that there is something in the carburettor, then it is the case that the situation is this way and not another way. Positive replies as much as negative replies introduce non-being into the undifferentiated fullness of being-in-itself.

For Sartre, then, the world of phenomena we are conscious of is not determined by being but by negation. That this is so can be revealed in various ways.

It is useful to ask what is involved in the appearance of an entity as distinct from other entities. With regard to their being, all entities are the same. That is, at the level of being there are no entities. Being, in and of itself, cannot realize the differentiation required for entities to appear. The appearance of an entity, the appearance of a distinct this, must always be the appearance of a figure on a ground.[12]

Crucially, it is consciousness that causes the entity to appear as a figure on a ground by negating the ground.

Further evidence of Sartre's deep-rooted transcendental idealism is his view of the phenomenon of motion. He notes that an object in motion never occupies an exact location, not even for a moment. To suppose that a moving object occupies an exact location at any particular time is to claim that as it moves it is at rest. Apart from the obvious contradiction involved in the notion that motion is comprised of moments of rest, it is a notion that precludes an explanation of how an object moves from point A at time $T1$ to point B at time $T2$. Arguing that an object passes from point A to point B by passing through a number of intermediate points achieves nothing because it does not explain how the object passes from one intermediate point to the next. Sartre's response to the problem of motion – a problem first raised, though not answered, by the pre-Socratic philosopher Zeno of Elea[13] – is to take up once again the position of a transcendental idealist and argue that motion is for consciousness. An object in motion, he claims, is where it is not and is not where it is. As noted, this paradox also applies to being-for-itself. Describing movement, he writes:

> It is simultaneously to be at a place and not to be there. At no moment can it be said that the being of the passage is here, without running the risk of abruptly stopping it there, but neither can it be said that it is not, or that it is not there, or that it is elsewhere. Its relation with the place is not a relation of occupation. (*BN*, p. 211)

These remarks seem absurd unless it is appreciated that for Sartre motion is for consciousness. An object in motion is an object perpetually exterior to itself. As it moves it is perpetually no longer where it was and not yet where it will be. This no-longer and not-yet cannot belong to the object itself. They are negations that must be ascribed to it by consciousness, as its very objectness must be ascribed to it by consciousness: 'the relation of the moving body to itself is a pure relation of indifference and can be revealed only to a witness' (*BN*, p. 212). For Sartre, then, there is only motion for consciousness. The undifferentiatedness of being-in-itself, as he conceives it, is such that there can be no movement within being-in-itself. Movement requires differentiation, which is always from the point of view of consciousness, for there even to be entities that can shift location relative to one another.

Challenging Sartre's transcendental idealism, it might simply be asked: 'Why, if there is no motion apart from consciousness, do we constantly discover objects in a different place from where we last saw them?' Surely, objects do undergo what can only be described as motion apart from consciousness. This objection is so simple it seems it must miss Sartre's point, yet perhaps it is Sartre himself, when he argues as he does on the subject of motion, who is missing the point. Granted, he is offering an ingenious solution to an ancient philosophical problem, but arguably he loses his usual healthy sense of reality in the process. The root of the problem is that when Sartre is in his transcendental idealist mode he will allow nothing whatsoever on the side of being-in-itself except that it is. He insists that undifferentiated being is non-temporal, non spatial, objectless, contains no motion and has no properties or relations of any kind. Recall Hegel's view that pure being and pure nothing are one and the same. In the final analysis, Sartre's undifferentiated being also seems to amount to pure nothing.

Can the world, apart from our consciousness of it, really be so completely undifferentiated? Surely, the world has its own processes, patterns and motions quite apart from us. Natural phenomena, such as plants and animals, have their own patterns of existence that do not require our interest in order to occur. Granted, the world we encounter is characterized in all sorts of ways by us. There is a definite sense in which the world is our world. To argue, however, that without the involvement of consciousness there is simply no world of phenomena at all is an extreme anthropocentrism that disregards the evidence of nature. What inspires this extreme view? Partly, it is a desire to reverse the Copernican revolution by placing us back at the centre of the universe – conceptually rather than astronomically. The main motive, however, is to answer an ancient question regarding phenomena: 'If this chair is a chair for me, what is it and what remains of it as a chair when it is not a chair for me?' Unfortunately, attempting to answer this question in the terms of transcendental idealism gives rise to a crass disregard for the robust life of its own of mind-independent reality. Mind-independent reality is denied everything except its being.

Having considered both Sartre's realism and Sartre's transcendental idealism, I can offer answers to a couple of questions raised earlier: (1) which of Sartre's two agendas is the more intelligible, realism or transcendental idealism? and (2) which is more deeply rooted in the structure of his thought?

To answer the second question first: it is transcendental idealism that is the more deeply rooted in Sartre's thought. It is inseparable from his fundamental ontology. Transcendental idealism is unavoidably implied by his view of the relationship between being and nonbeing that lies at the very heart of his system. Sartre quite clearly holds that being-in-itself is undifferentiated and that phenomena arise entirely through the negation of being.

In answer to the other question, it seems that Sartre's realism is the more intelligible of his two agendas, but perhaps that is only because it appeals to common sense more than his transcendental idealism. It is tempting to say that it makes perfect sense to suppose the world is out there in all its diversity quite apart from any consciousness of it, that it is not just formed out of undifferentiated being when consciousness arrives on the scene. Yet this view is not without difficulties of its own, even if it avoids those presented by Sartre's transcendental idealism. For instance, on what grounds can a person insist that the world is as it appears to him even when it is not appearing to him? He cannot know that the objects in his room do not collapse into undifferentiated being when he departs because by definition he cannot see the unseeable. There is, of course, a wealth of evidence to suggest that the world carries on behind his back, but this evidence cannot satisfy sceptics who argue that if a person finds the proverbial tree in the forest has fallen, he does not know it fell. All he knows (accepting that he can trust his senses) is that it is now lying where it once stood. Perhaps objects that move in his absence – supposing there are objects in his absence – do so by quantum leaps. He cannot be where he is not, and the impossibility of disproving that objects move by quantum leaps in his absence is the impossibility of being where he is not.

Perhaps, in the end, realism is the more intelligible position because it reflects the natural attitude of all but madmen, whereas transcendental idealism does not. Philosophers speculate endlessly as to the nature of reality apart from consciousness of it, but any description of reality cannot help assuming that phenomena are there as they appear to us, undergoing their own motions and processes quite apart from us. When Sartre is not directly concerned with the being of the phenomenon he too makes this assumption. He simply accepts the mind-independent reality of reality and gets on with describing the relationship we have with it, not in terms of its being for us, but in terms of its significance for us. Here, Sartre's aim is to consider how a café, for example, is characterized for a person by the absence of an expected friend, rather than to consider whether or not the café collapses into undifferentiated being when no one is conscious of it. 'It is certain that the café by itself with its patrons, its tables, its booths, its mirrors, its light, its smoky atmosphere . . . is a fullness of being' (*BN*, p. 9).

Sartre's position that all situations are interpreted according to their personal significance is a vital component of his phenomenology demanding closer consideration.

Sartre is unwavering in his view that a person interprets every situation according to his desires, hopes, expectations and intentions. Every situation a person encounters is understood as presently lacking something desired, expected, intended or anticipated. Of course, the situation in itself does not lack – in itself the situation is a fullness of being – the situation lacks something for the person in question. For Sartre, consciousness is always predisposed to find something lacking. Indeed, he maintains that lack is intrinsic to the very meaning of every situation for any particular consciousness. What are his reasons for maintaining this position?

Every situation, he argues, is a situation for the for-itself. The for-itself, as that which exists by negating the situation, must be situated in order to be. The for-itself, for which the situation is a situation, is not part of the situation, but the negation of the situation. It transcends the situation in order to realize the situation. Every situation is understood not in terms of what it is but in terms of what it lacks, and what every situation lacks is precisely the for-itself. The for-itself is those particular lacks that determine the situation as a situation. Sartre explores the phenomenon of lack through the example of judging that the moon is not full (*BN*, p. 86).

In itself a crescent moon is neither complete nor incomplete; it is simply what it is. In order to understand what it is – a partial appearance of the full moon – it must be judged in terms of the full moon that is presently lacking. The meaning of the crescent moon is founded upon the non-being of the full moon as that which the crescent moon lacks. The crescent moon itself does not lack the full moon. The crescent moon lacks the full moon for a consciousness that is the surpassing of the being of the crescent moon towards the non-being of the full moon. It is the non-being of the full moon that gives the crescent moon its meaning for consciousness. For consciousness the crescent moon exists in the mode of being the non-being of the full moon. As that which is given, the crescent moon is what it is. As a meaningful phenomenon, the crescent moon is understood as what it is by virtue of what it lacks. 'In order for this in-itself to be grasped as the crescent moon, it is necessary that a human reality surpass the given towards the project of the realised totality – here the disk of the full moon – and return toward the given to constitute it as the crescent moon' (*BN*, p. 86).

In so far as the for-itself is those particular lacks that determine the situation, it is itself a lack. Recall that the for-itself – unlike the in-itself – is that which can never achieve identity with itself. The for-itself is that which lacks identity with itself, or, to put it simply, the for-itself is that which lacks itself. 'The lack of the for-itself is a lack which it is. The outline of a presence-to-itself as that which is lacking to the for-itself is what constitutes the being of the for-itself as the foundation of its own nothingness' (*BN*, p. 101). This is not to say that the for-itself is a lack in itself. If it was a lack in itself it would be identical with itself as lack, whereas it is that which cannot achieve identity with itself either as being or as non-being. Its being is to be what it is not and not to be what it is. The for-itself has rather *to be* its own lack. As the negation of being the for-itself is a lack of being, but as the negation of itself as a lack of being it is that which strives in vain to lack itself as nothing in order to be being.

The lack that the for-itself has to be is revealed by desire and the fact that desire *per se* can never be satisfied. That is, although a person can satisfy a particular desire by obtaining the object of that desire, any particular satisfaction is immediately surpassed towards a further desire. The lack that the for-itself has to be manifests itself in the form of a desire for something presently lacked. The for-itself, as that which perpetually strives to become for-itself-in-itself, hopes to be united with the object of its desire when that object is obtained. 'If only I possessed her', sighs the lover, 'I would never want for anything again', fooling himself that by possessing his beloved he would achieve the impossible and become a permanently fulfilled lack. Constituted as a lack that it has to be, the for-itself cannot be fulfilled. As the negation of being it must surpass any particular obtained object of desire towards a further unobtained object of desire.[14] 'Hence the constant disappointment which accompanies repletion, the famous: "Is it only this?" which is not directed at the concrete pleasure which satisfaction gives but at the evanescence of the coincidence with self' (*BN*, pp. 101–2).

From the fact that the complete satisfaction of all desire is unachievable, Sartre concludes pessimistically that everyone experiences constant disappointment. Is this a reasonable conclusion to draw? Disappointment is certainly common, with people and events frequently failing to live up to expectations, but there are also occasions when people and events exceed expectations and satisfaction is achieved. Adopting the tragic view of life of the existentialist writer, Sartre claims in his novel *Nausea* that 'there are no perfect moments' (*N*, p. 213). This may be so for people who have sunk to the level of pessimism and self-absorption of the novel's main character, but many other less pessimistic and self-absorbed people claim to have experienced at least a few perfect moments in their lives: moments of pure excitement or delight when dissatisfaction was temporarilly forgotten. Sartre argues that there are no perfect moments not least because time flies rendering coincidence with self impossible. He sometimes suggests, nonetheless, that the very transience of a moment can perfect it:

> So there, at one and the same time, you had that fence which smells so strongly of wet wood, that lantern, and that little blonde in the Negro's arms, under a fiery-coloured sky . . . all those soft colours, the beautiful blue coat which looked like an eiderdown, the light-coloured raincoat, the red panes of the lantern . . . the whole scene came alive for me with a significance which was strong and even fierce, but pure. Then it broke up, and nothing remained but the lantern, the fence, and the sky: it was still quite beautiful. An hour later, the lantern was lit, the wind was blowing, the sky was dark: nothing at all was left. (*N*, p. 18)

The issue of satisfaction raises many more questions than can be answered here. What does it mean to say that a person is satisfied? Does a person have temporarily to lose awareness of himself in order to achieve true satisfaction? Whatever the answers to these questions, it seems reasonable to claim that for many the experience of dissatisfaction is not as intense or as constant as Sartre suggests. A person may discover on reflection that he is a 'useless passion' (*BN*, p. 615), but he does not always feel that he is. Or is the opposite the case?

A person feels he is a useless passion moment by moment, but on reflection he convinces himself that he is not; that he was not. Sartre favours the latter view when he writes: 'for the most commonplace event to become an adventure, you must – and this is all that is necessary – start *recounting* it' (*N*, p. 61). Perhaps the moment in the street described above was not perfect when it took place. It was not pure; recounting it purified it. Perhaps the narrator is simply being nostalgic, forgetting that at the time he had cares that infected the moment with imperfection.

Closely associated with the phenomenon of existential lack is the phenomenon of existential absence. Sartre outlines existential absence by describing the experience of discovering that his friend is absent from the café where he has arranged to meet him (*BN*, pp. 9–10): 'When I enter this café to search for Pierre, there is formed a synthetic organization of all the objects in the café, on the ground of which Pierre is given as about to appear' (*BN*, p. 9). Pierre, as the person Sartre expects to find, is existentially absent. This existential absence is distinct from an abstract and purely formal absence that is merely thought. '. . . "Wellington is not in this café, Paul Valéry is no longer here, etc." – these have a purely abstract meaning; they are pure applications of the principle of negation without real or efficacious foundation, and they never succeed in establishing a real relation between the café and Wellington or Valéry' (*BN*, p. 10). The distinction between existential and formal absence emphasizes that non-being does not arise through judgements made by consciousness after encountering the world, but that non-being belongs to the very nature of the world as it is for consciousness. Pierre's absence from the café is not merely thought. His absence is an actual event at the café that characterizes the café as the place from which Pierre is absent. For the person expecting Pierre, the café has no other significant character until Pierre presents himself: 'my expectation has caused the absence of Pierre to *happen* as a real event concerning this café' (*BN*, p. 10).

It can be objected that Sartre's love of the dramatic leads him to exaggerate. Just because Pierre is absent from the café it does not follow that the person expecting him is doomed to experience the café and everyone in it as the neutral background to Pierre's absence. The person expecting Pierre could be aware of expecting him, yet still enjoy the café in the meantime. Sartre might concede that he has exaggerated the level of expectation experienced by a balanced person whose friend is a little late. He would insist, however, that if a person is particularly eager or desperate for another to arrive then the experience of their absence will be as he describes it. Ultimately, Sartre convinces us of the reality of existential absence as he describes it because we can all identify with his description to some degree through our own experience. It would be an unusually indifferent person who could not relate to the experience he describes.

A person's entire world can exist in the mode of the negative; in the mode of not being the presence of whatever is desired. The misery of missing someone or something is rooted in this negating of the world. For a withdrawing heroin addict, for example, the pain of physical withdrawal lasts only a few days. The misery of psychological withdrawal, however, lasts much longer and arises from the addict's experience of the whole world as the flat, monotonous absence of a fix. Nothing interests or inspires a withdrawing addict except that absent fix. Even things that have no direct association with heroin refer the addict to heroin simply because they are not heroin. The addict's entire world is reduced to not being heroin. Similarly, the misery of losing a lover lies not so much in the loss of the pleasure the lover gave, but in the reduction of everything to a dull background that has no other significance or value than to be the perpetual affirmation of the lover's absence.

A person can often be more significant in his absence than in his presence. Presence reduces a person to the limits of his physical stature; whereas absence can transfigure a person in the minds of others. He can become almost omnipresent in his absence. Sartre claims to have been struck by this phenomenon as a child. In *Words*, the autobiography of his early life, he writes:

> my grandfather, from the height of his glory, made a pronouncement which pierced me to the heart: 'Someone's lacking here: it's Simonnot.' . . . This astonishing absence transfigured him. A great many people connected with the Institute were absent . . . but these were accidental and trifling facts. Only Monsieur Simonnot was *lacking*. It had been enough to mention his name: emptiness had sunk into that crowded hall like a knife. I was amazed that a man had his place fixed. His place: a void hollowed out by universal expectation. (*W*, p. 58)

Nowhere is Sartre's view that the significance of the world is its significance for each person more emphatically expressed than in his consideration of the phenomenon of destruction. Sartre argues that it is only for a consciousness, for a witness, that entities are destroyed: 'man is the only being by whom a destruction can be accomplished. A geological plication, a storm do not destroy – at least they do not destroy *directly*; they merely modify the distribution of masses of beings' (*BN*, p. 8).

Sartre's comments on destruction – which could also apply to creation – are straightforward and uncontentious when taken in the following way: a city is destroyed for people because only people can experience its loss as significant. Outside of their evaluation of the situation nothing has been destroyed, in the sense that there is as much matter remaining after an earthquake as there was before. Sartre, however, is saying more than this. He is making the more contentious claim that destruction requires a witness who is capable of positing the non-being – the no-longer-being – of destroyed entities. When a cup breaks, for example, there is as much china as there was before it broke. Nonetheless, the cup has ceased to be. The requisite cup-shape has gone, along with its capacity to fulfil a certain function. It is these qualities – qualities that exist for drinkers – that constitute the being of the cup, not the material of which the cup is made. The qualities, of course, require the material and cannot be separated from it. Rearrange the material and the qualities become nothing, except for a consciousness that can retain them in their nothingness in the mode of *was*: 'to posit otherness there must be a witness who can retain the past in some manner and compare it to the present in the form of *no longer*' (*BN*, p. 8).

Once again, Sartre is attempting to account for phenomena via transcendental idealism. As the example of the cup shows, the problem of what constitutes phenomena is a real one. It is a problem to which I can see no obvious solution; suffice it to say that to seek to solve it via transcendental idealism is to raise another problem already considered: the problem of the apparent incoherence of the claim that being is completely undifferentiated apart from consciousness of it. It is beyond the scope of this book to solve the problem of phenomena as illustrated by the example of the cup, while simultaneously avoiding the apparently incoherent claim that being is completely undifferentiated apart from consciousness of it. It is tempting to suggest that if being is differentiated apart from consciousness of it, then it is differentiated by virtue of universal metaphysical forms that give reality to particular things.[15]

Unfortunately, searching for answers along these lines reintroduces many metaphysical difficulties that the anti-metaphysical approach of existential phenomenology appears to overcome.

CONSCIOUSNESS AND TEMPORALITY

The being of the for-itself is to be what it is not and not to be what it is. Only an essentially temporal being can have this paradoxical nature lacking self-identity. Understanding temporality shows how such a nature is possible: 'the *cogito* refuses instantaneity . . . this can happen only within a temporal surpassing . . . we can not hope to elucidate the being of the for-itself until we have described and determined the significance of the Temporal' (*BN*, pp. 104–5). Sartre agrees with Heidegger's crucial claim that '*the central problematic of all ontology is rooted in the phenomenon of time*' (Heidegger 1993, p. 40).[16] Moreover, Sartre's account of the temporality of the for-itself draws heavily upon Heidegger's account of the temporality of *Dasein* and is markedly similar to it. Heidegger's position is therefore worth considering.

Heidegger notes that it is essential to the being of every person that they be situated. Situatedness is a person's essential way of being. Heidegger's term for this essential way of being is *Dasein*. The most common translation of *Dasein* from the German is 'being-there'. However, although *sein* certainly means 'being', *Da* does not always mean 'there'. *Da* can mean 'neither here nor there, but somewhere in between'. *Dasein* has been translated as 'being-here', but this formulation is no more exact, in that it ignores the 'there' aspect of Da. Quibbling over the exact meaning of *Da* is useful because it reveals the being of *Dasein* as that which is neither here nor there. *Dasein* is essentially indeterminate.

As noted, an object in motion never occupies an exact location. Its exact location at any moment is indeterminate. If it occupied an exact location at any particular moment as it moved then it would be at rest. Therefore, an object in motion must be neither here nor there. A basic understanding of the indeterminate being of *Dasein* can be gained by comparing it with an object in motion, although this is only an analogy. The essential 'motion' of *Dasein* – its essential indeterminacy – is not spatial but temporal. *Dasein* is essentially temporal. As an essentially temporal movement away from the past towards the future, *Dasein* temporalizes being. Temporality is the meaning that *Dasein* gives to being and is, therefore, the meaning of being as it is for *Dasein*. The temporality that *Dasein* recognizes as an essential feature of being is nothing but its own temporalizing of being – the temporalizing that *Dasein* is. The temporality of being and the temporality of *Dasein* are one and the same.

As noted, Heidegger's concept of *Dasein* and Sartre's concept of the for-itself are closely related. Just as Heidegger's *Dasein* (being-here/there) is temporally neither here nor there, so Sartre's for-itself, as a perpetual flight towards the future, is also temporally neither here nor there.

Although it would be misleading to say that the for-itself is temporality, it is nonetheless by virtue of the for-itself that the world is temporalized. Time appears in the world through the negation of being that is the for-itself. As the negation of being, the for-itself must be a perpetual flight from being. But also, as that which must be its own negation, the for-itself must be a flight towards being. In short, the for-itself flees being towards being. This can be stated in specifically temporal terms: the for-itself flees being in the present towards being in the future. If the for-itself did not flee being in the present – did not perpetually make the present past – it would coincide with itself in the present. If it coincided with itself in the present it would become a being in itself, and as such would be annihilated as the non-being for itself which it has to be. Hence, the for-itself projects itself towards being in the future. The for-itself, however, can no more coincide with itself in the future than it can coincide with itself in the present. The for-itself cannot coincide with what is not yet, and when the future becomes the present, the for-itself, as a perpetual flight from being in the present, will already have flown this new present; it will already have made of this new present a past future.

It is important to recognize that that there is no such thing as the present. Indeed, neither are there such things as the past and the future. As is commonly noted, the past is no longer and the future is not yet. The correct way to view time is not in terms of three distinct and substantial elements, but in terms of three unified dimensions, each of which, being nothing in itself, is outside of itself in the other two and has meaning only in terms of the other two. Sartre refers to this structure as *ekstatic*, and to each of the three dimensions of time as an *ekstasis* (*BN*, p. 137).[17] The future is referred to as a future-past, while the past is referred to as a past-future. As for the present, it is the immediate presence of the for-itself to being, rather than a present moment that can be considered as being *now*. There is, strictly speaking, no such thing as now. *NOW!* can never hit its target. As to what is ordinarily described as 'the here and now', it is the situation to which the for-itself is presence; the situation that the for-itself realizes by perpetually surpassing it towards the future.

> it would be absurd to say that it is nine o'clock for the for-itself, but the for-itself can be present to a hand pointed at nine o'clock. What we falsely call the Present is the being to which the present is presence. It is impossible to grasp the Present in the form of an instant, for the instant would be the moment when the present *is*. But the present is not; it makes itself present in the form of flight. (*BN*, p. 123)

The for-itself is a flight towards the future. It is a flight that realizes the past and the future as its past and future. It is a flight by which the future is constituted as a future-past and the past as a past-future. It is a flight by which the future becomes the past. There are two immediate conclusions to be drawn from this:

1. Being-in-itself is not temporalized. It is only for the for-itself which flees it towards the future that being is temporalized. It is only for the for-itself that being, apparent as differentiated being, is apprehended as not yet being what it will be and as no longer being what it was.
2. The non-being of the present and the non-being of the for-itself are one and the same: 'the present is for-itself' (*BN*, p. 120).

The present belongs to the immediate structure of the for-itself and as such is nothing in itself. It is not a continual subjective now or a series of subjective nows in which the for-itself is present to itself. Neither is it a continual objective now or a series of objective nows in which the in-itself is present to itself in the form of a moment-by-moment at-present of objects that is then comprehended by the mind. The present has no being of its own. It is not a real or metaphysical condition of the world or the mind but is rather the presence of the for-itself to the in-itself.

What is the fundamental meaning of the present? It is clear that what exists in the present is distinguished from all other existence by the characteristic of presence. At roll-call the soldier or the pupil replies 'Present!' in the form of *adsum*. Present is opposed to absent as well as to past. Thus the meaning of the present is presence to ___. . . . A being which is present to ___ can not be at rest 'in-itself'; the in-itself can not be present anymore than it can be Past. It simply is . . . The present therefore can be only the presence of the For-itself to being-in-itself . . . The For-itself is defined as presence to being. (*BN*, pp. 120–1)

Concluding his argument that the present has precisely the same self-identity-lacking and paradoxical nature as the for-itself, Sartre restates his maxim that the being of the for-itself is not to be what it is and is to be what it is not in specifically temporal terms: 'At present it [the for-itself] is not what it is (past) and it is what it is not (future)' (*BN*, p. 123).

The present must be equated with the for-itself and defined negatively. Equating the for-itself with the present and describing it in temporal terms reveals the sense of the apparently absurd claim that the for-itself is not what it is and is what it is not. If the for-itself was a self-identical positivity instead of an express negation then human reality would be impossible. The experience of being is possible only for a being that is not being, a being that experiences itself as a relation to a being that it is not. As the negation of being the for-itself cannot be co-present with being-in-itself, otherwise its temporal flight would be arrested and it would be reduced to being-in-itself. Co-presence, rather than being the co-presence of the for-itself and the in-itself, is a relationship between objects from the point of view of the for-itself when the for-itself is equally present to them. 'This table must be present to that chair in a world which human reality haunts as a presence' (*BN*, p. 121).

That the for-itself cannot be co-present with being implies temporality. As noted, the for-itself flees being towards the future. That it does so is an immediate and necessary feature of the for-itself. Indeed, the for-itself is this perpetual flight. Metaphorically speaking, the for-itself, like a photon, has no rest mass. The future towards which the for-itself flees is the always future possibility of its becoming for-itself-in-itself. An always future possibility that is always impossible at present. The for-itself is that which aims at being for-itself-in-itself without ever being able to be it. And it cannot be it for the simple reason that the negation of being cannot also be a fullness of being. The for-itself is, and must be, a lack of itself in the present.

The temporality of the self is as central to Sartre's philosophy as it is to Heidegger's, and there is a significant degree of convergence in their views. Nevertheless, it is worth considering an important difference between them on the subject.

Unlike Sartre, who makes extensive use of the term 'consciousness', Heidegger avoids it. He avoids it because, in his view, it implies that a person's essential way of being is passively to contemplate being, when in fact a person's essential way of being is actively to question being. Heidegger prefers the term *Dasein*, believing that it better captures a person's essential way of being. So far, the difference between them is unimportant because just as in speaking of *Dasein* Heidegger is not denying that a person is aware of being and capable of contemplating it, in speaking of 'consciousness' Sartre is not denying that a person's essential way of being is actively to question being. However, in bypassing consciousness in favour of *Dasein* for his own good reasons, Heidegger also bypasses the original negation that for Sartre constitutes the very being of consciousness at the ontological level. For Sartre, the fact that the original negation is the negation of being-in-itself affirms the ontological priority of being over non-being. In bypassing the original negation Heidegger fails to recognize what Sartre identifies: that it is the original negation as a perpetual passing beyond being that gives rise to temporality, and that temporality must, therefore, be ontologically subsequent to being. Sartre, it seems, provides an adequate account of the ontological origin of the temporality of the self, whereas Heidegger does not.[18]

Sartre's phenomenology, as noted, swings between realism and transcendental idealism. Before concluding this section, it is worth considering Sartre's view of temporality in the light of this ambiguity. Sartre sometimes suggests that the temporalizing of being by consciousness is further evidence that being is completely undifferentiated apart from consciousness. However, it can be consistently argued both that consciousness temporalizes being and that there is a world of phenomena in process apart from consciousness. To argue (as Sartre does consistently) that there is no time apart from consciousness is not to argue (as Sartre does sometimes) that apart from consciousness there is no becoming, that without consciousness nothing comes into or goes out of existence. It is simply to argue that apart from consciousness there is no awareness of the process of becoming; no positing of a past or future for any particular present. For example, as it is in itself quite apart from anyone being conscious of it, an acorn is in process of becoming an oak. Yet an acorn is not thereby aiming at becoming an oak. It is not projecting itself towards any future goal and has no futurizing intention by means of which it recognizes itself as that which presently lacks itself as an oak tree. In the sense that becoming an oak is not a project for the acorn, it is correct to say that the acorn has no future. It has a future only for a consciousness that understands that the acorn is not yet an oak but will be an oak in future. If the claim that there is no time apart from consciousness is understood in this way then it does not amount to an argument against realism. Understood in this way, claiming that there is no time apart from consciousness is not equivalent to claiming that nothing happens apart from consciousness. Rather, it is equivalent to claiming that apart from consciousness the world is without the phenomena of no-longer and not-yet.

SELF-CONSCIOUSNESS

Sartre's views on self-consciousness are vital to his theory of consciousness as a whole. Sartre holds that there are two modes of self-consciousness: non-thetic consciousness (of) consciousness and thetic self-consciousness. Strictly speaking, the former should not be referred to as 'self-consciousness' because it does not involve the for-itself contemplating itself as an intentional object. The latter is self-consciousness as ordinarily understood: consciousness reflecting on itself and taking itself as the intentional object of its contemplation.

Non-thetic consciousness (of) consciousness is implicit, non-positional, pre-reflective, pre-reflexive consciousness.[19] It is a necessary condition of positional consciousness of intentional objects. Without non-thetic, pre-reflective consciousness (of) consciousness the for-itself would not be conscious because to be conscious is to be conscious of being so. In *The Transcendence of the Ego* Sartre writes: 'the object with its characteristic opacity is before consciousness, but consciousness is purely and simply consciousness of being conscious of that object. This is the law of its existence' (*TE*, p. 40). Non-thetic consciousness (of) consciousness is not a separate act of consciousness that is brought to bear on positional consciousness of intentional objects. It is an internal and essential feature of positional consciousness without which positional consciousness could not be. Non-thetic consciousness (of) consciousness exists by virtue of the translucency of consciousness. As nothing but consciousness of intentional objects, consciousness is consciousness through and through; it is without opacity. Non-thetic consciousness (of) consciousness belongs, therefore, to the very being of consciousness as that which is utterly translucent. Consciousness that is not non-thetically and pre-reflectively conscious of itself is impossible because consciousness is consciousness (of) being conscious of objects.

Sartre's case seems a strong one. It is difficult to conceive of a situation in which there could be consciousness of x without there being consciousness (of) consciousness of x. Or is it so difficult? John can be conscious that Jane looks angry, but not be conscious that this is because she has wide eyes, flushed cheeks and pursed lips. Such situations undoubtedly occur. However, doubt is cast upon Sartre's assertions regarding the impossibility of consciousness that is not non-thetically conscious only if, in asserting that consciousness of Jane's anger is consciousness (of) being conscious of Jane's anger, he is also asserting that consciousness of Jane's anger is consciousness of all the particulars that comprise the general impression. But Sartre does not assert the latter when he asserts the former. He simply asserts that to be conscious of Jane's anger, John must be non-thetically conscious (of) his consciousness of Jane's anger. This assertion says nothing, and need say nothing, about John's consciousness, or lack of it, of the particulars that give rise to his consciousness of Jane's anger.

The other mode of self-consciousness, thetic consciousness of consciousness, is positional, explicit and reflective self-consciousness. It is self-consciousness as ordinarily understood. It is self-reflection. To avoid confusion it has not been said until now that positional consciousness of intentional objects is also known as thetic consciousness. Thetic consciousness, as positional consciousness of intentional objects, is capable of positional consciousness of itself as an intentional object. This positional consciousness of consciousness is thetic self-consciousness, or what Sartre often refers to as reflective consciousness or the reflective.

It is important to note that reflective consciousness is non-thetically conscious (of) itself. Sartre argues that non-thetic consciousness (of) consciousness is an internal and essential feature of all acts of consciousness. It follows, therefore, that non-thetic consciousness (of) consciousness must also be an internal and essential feature of reflective consciousness: 'the reflective [thetic self-consciousness] is *witness* of the reflected-on without thereby ceasing to be an appearance to itself . . . the reflective can be witness only in so far as it is consciousness (of) being so' (*BN*, p. 152).

Describing self-consciousness solely in terms of the reflective act by which consciousness takes itself as an intentional object is unsatisfactory because it gives no account of consciousness (of) reflective consciousness. To assume that self-consciousness consists only of reflective consciousness is to posit an impossible situation in which reflective consciousness lacks consciousness (of) itself. Without nonthetic consciousness (of) reflective consciousness, reflective consciousness cannot occur. Non-thetic consciousness (of) reflective consciousness is a necessary condition of reflective consciousness without which reflective consciousness would not be conscious.

It has been noted that non-thetic consciousness is not separate from thetic consciousness. Similarly, thetic self-consciousness or reflective consciousness is not separate from the consciousness reflected on. However, it is incorrect to infer from this that reflective and reflected-on consciousness are identical. In truth, their relationship is paradoxical. It is in developing an account of the paradoxical relationship between reflective and reflected-on consciousness that the best sense of reflective consciousness can be made.

Reflective and reflected-on consciousness are not and cannot be two independent phenomena. 'how can two completely isolated independents, provided with that sufficiency of being which the Germans call *Selbständigkeit*, enter into relation with each other, and in particular how can they enter into that type of internal relation which we call knowledge?' (*BN*, p. 151). Knowledge or knowing is the internal negation of the known. The knower is nothing beyond the negation of the known. The relation between reflective and reflected-on consciousness, therefore, must be internal and not external. Just as the pre-reflective consciousness reflected-on is internally related to the world of which it is conscious, so reflective consciousness is internally related to reflected-on consciousness. Reflection is not one for-itself reflecting on another for-itself within an individual person, as though the person consisted of two externally related for-itselves. Rather, reflection is the for-itself conscious of itself. This relation of the for-itself to itself requires an absence of identity as much as it requires an absence of independence. Identity would prevent the for-itself from knowing itself as much as independence would. Therefore, 'it is necessary that the reflective simultaneously be and not be the reflected-on' (BN, p. 151). This ontological structure is familiar. As seen, it lies at the very heart of the for-itself. The for-itself, as that which exists at a distance from itself, is capable of being an appearance for itself. It is capable of witnessing itself.

The for-itself is the nihilation (the negation) of being. Reflection is the nihilation of the for-itself by itself. Sartre asks: 'Where is the origin of this further negation? What can be its motivation?' (BN, p. 153). The origin of this further nihilation is a further attempt on the part of the for-itself to cease being what it is not and not what it is, and to become what it is. This further attempt on the part of the for-itself to be what it is is central to the project of bad faith. The for-itself in bad faith exploits the possibility of reflective consciousness to consider itself as a self-identical being, even though it would not be capable of reflection if this self-identity was realized. By reflecting upon itself, the for-itself attempts to establish itself as a given: as an objective consciousness in itself that witnesses itself as such. This project is doomed to failure not least because the for-itself cannot witness itself unless it is at a distance from itself. Reflection aims to render the for-itself identical with itself, but achieving reflection requires that the for-itself be other than itself.

> This effort to be to itself its own foundation, to recover and to dominate within itself its own flight, finally to be that flight instead of temporalizing it as the flight which is fled – this effort inevitably results in failure; and it is precisely this failure which is reflection. In fact it is itself the being which has to recover the being which is lost, and it must be this recovery in the mode of being which is its own; that is, in the mode of the for-itself, therefore of flight. (BN, p. 154)

As noted, the for-itself is essentially temporal. It follows, therefore, that the reflection of the for-itself upon itself has temporal dimensions. The for-itself reflected-on is always past for the reflective for-itself because the reflective for-itself flees the for-itself reflected-on towards the future in order to attempt to fix it in the present. The for-itself reflected-on appears as present to the reflective for-itself. It appears as a for-itself present in-itself, all at once; a temporal flight recovered and condensed into an instant. To the reflective for-itself, the for-itself reflected-on appears as a for-itself-in-itself. This, of course, is a mere appearance, because the reflective for-itself is the for-itself exterior to itself. The for-itself must be exterior to itself in order to reflect upon itself as an apparent for-itself-in-itself. Not least, the appearance of the for-itself reflected-on as a for-itself-in-itself has to be perpetually renewed by the reflective for-itself. A genuine for-itself-in-itself (which is impossible) would maintain itself and would not have to be perpetually renewed in this way.

The appearance of the for-itself reflected-on as a for-itself-in-itself for the reflective for-itself is the ontological basis of the appearance of the psyche, ego or 'I' as an intentional object that endures through time. 'A psychic fact is then the shadow of the reflected-on inasmuch as the reflective has to be it ekstatically in the mode of non-being' (*BN*, p. 161). The for-itself reflected-on appears to the reflective for-itself as a present, intentional, transcendent object. Through reflection, particular fleeting phases of the for-itself as it is in its immediate relation to the world – reactions, aversions, desires and so on – appear as aspects of present, transcendent psychic objects – love, hate, hope, fear, and so on.[20] In turn, these psychic objects appear as aspects of a present and enduring ego posited by reflection as the supposed underlying unity of these psychic objects.

What is revealed to it [the reflective for-itself] is not the temporal and non-substantial historicity of the reflected-on; [rather] beyond this reflected-on it is the very substantiality of the organized forms of the flow. The unity of these virtual beings is called the *psychic life* or the *psyche*, a virtual and transcendent in-itself which underlies the temporalization of the for-itself. (*BN*, pp. 161–2)

Similar thoughts are expressed in Sartre's *The Transcendence of the Ego*. Concerned to distinguish the ego or psyche from consciousness, Sartre argues that the ego is an appearance for reflective consciousness existing entirely as the transcendent unity of previous states and actions: 'Undoubtedly, it [the ego] is transcendent to all the states which it unifies, but not as an abstract X whose mission is only to unify: rather, it is the infinite totality of states and of actions which is never reducible to *an* action or to *a* state' (*TE*, p. 74).

CHAPTER 2

BEING-FOR-OTHERS

. . . I need the Other in order to realize fully all the structures of my being. The For-itself refers to the For-others.

(*BN*, p. 222)

So far I have considered the various structures of human subjectivity as the transcendent negation of being. That is, the various structures of being-for-itself. There is, however, a further aspect of human subjectivity to be considered if I am to proceed to a satisfactory account of freedom and bad faith. This further aspect of human subjectivity is being-for-others. Being-for-others accounts for certain ontologically distinct modes of consciousness that cannot be accounted for simply in terms of being-for-itself. One such mode of consciousness is shame.

Shame is *for* consciousness, and a person is ashamed in so far as he is conscious of shame. However, although shame is a structure of the self a person does not realize it for himself and by himself.[1] Shame requires a direct apprehension of another person (the Other) as a being who sees me. 'Shame is not originally a phenomenon of reflection . . . it is in its primary structure shame *before somebody*' (*BN*, p. 221). To understand what is involved in being seen as an experience that is not merely comprehended but lived is to understand the meaning and significance of being-for-others.

Human beings are objects. They have bodies, objects that are externally related to other objects and which are affected by the same physical determinants that affect all objects. However, although human beings are objects and the Other is a human being, it is not as an object that the Other is originally revealed to me. Sartre develops his view of the way in which the Other is revealed to me by exploring the phenomenon of encounter through a range of concrete examples.

Sartre's first concrete example is not one in which the Other encounters me, but one in which I simply see another person who does not see me (*BN*, p. 254). The purpose of this example is to outline certain structures that will help elucidate the central case Sartre is interested in: that of being encountered. I see a man in an otherwise empty park. Immediately, my awareness of the man's presence in the park affects my situation. The man's appearance constitutes the start of the disintegration of the world from my own point of view. Suddenly, the situation, which was mine to evaluate as I pleased, contains a new source of values which are not mine and which escape me. 'The appearance of the Other in the world corresponds to a fixed sliding of the whole universe, to a decentralization of the world which undermines the centralization which I am simultaneously effecting' (*BN*, p. 255).

The reorientation of the world towards the man, the fact that meanings unknown to me flow in his direction, constitutes him as a drain-hole into which my own world flows. This is why a person seeking the joys of solitude in the wilds might feel annoyed when he sees another person, even if that other person does not see him. The very appearance of another person prevents him from playing God. He ceases to be the centre and sole judge of all he surveys because a source of re-evaluation has appeared on the scene to steal the world away from him and with it his glorious Godlike supremacy. A desert in which a person enjoying solitude encounters a stranger can feel more crowded than a busy street.

At this stage, the Other is still only a special kind of object. Although he is a drain-hole in my world and a threat to the centralization I effect, he remains an object in my world. However, that he is recognized as a threat to my centralization suggests that there are occasions when this threat is realized; occasions when he effects a radical reorientation of my being. In describing this radical reorientation, Sartre offers the following example: he invites us to imagine that he is a jealous, curious or corrupt person who, finding himself alone, listens at a door and spies through the keyhole (*BN*, p. 259). He is completely absorbed in his voyeuristic activities: 'I am a pure consciousness of things . . . My consciousness sticks to my acts, it *is* my acts, and my acts are commanded by the ends to be attained' (*BN*, p. 259). While absorbed in his actions, he does not judge them.

He does not know his actions, he is them. 'But all of a sudden I hear footsteps in the hall. Someone is looking at me! What does this mean? It means that I am suddenly affected in my being and that essential modifications appear in my structure' (*BN*, p. 260). Before considering the essential modifications that being looked at (the look) brings about, it must be noted that in order to experience himself as seen, a person need not be directly aware of another person's eyes turned in his direction. Consider the above example again: simply hearing footsteps in the hall can be enough for a person to experience himself as seen: 'the look will be given just as well on occasion when there is a rustling of branches, or the sound of a footstep followed by silence, or the slight opening of a shutter, or a light movement of a curtain' (*BN*, p. 257).

As noted, in the mode of for-itself the self is precisely not an object. It is a surpassing negation of being that is founded upon a being that it is not. It is not in the world as objects are but as a transcendence. Following Heidegger, Sartre refers to this mode of being as being-in-the-world. Being-in-the-world refers to a person's being for himself as 'the being which causes there to be a world by projecting itself beyond the world towards its own possibilities' (*BN*, p. 58). For himself, a person is not a thing alongside other things. He is not in being. Rather, he is that which freely transcends being towards the future. Being-in-the-world refers to the transcendent aspect of his being. The self, however, has another mode of being that Sartre, again following Heidegger, refers to as being-in-the-midst-of-the-world. Being-in-the-midst-of-the-world refers to a person's presence in the world as an object among other objects. Here, his free transcendence is transcended by the Other and he becomes a thing alongside other things. He is still his possibilities, but these possibilities are now a given fact for the Other. They belong also to the Other and are subject to the Other's judgement. This mode of being corresponds to a person's being-for-others and is realized when he experiences himself as seen by the Other or when he regards himself from the point of view of the Other.

Sartre argues that when a person experiences himself as seen by the Other he immediately ceases to be a transcendent subject, a pure point of view upon the world, and becomes instead an object in the midst of the world seen from the point of view of the Other. To experience himself as an object for the Other is to experience the Other as a subject. It is this direct and unmediated experience of himself as an object for the Other's subjectivity that reveals the Other to him as Other. He experiences the Other through the immediate, internal negation of his own transcendent subjectivity by the transcendent subjectivity of the Other. To experience the Other is for a person to exist his own being as a transcendence transcended: 'The other as a look is only that – my transcendence transcended' (*BN*, p. 263).

Returning to the example of the spy at the keyhole. So long as he is not caught in the act he remains a transcendence. That is, he perpetually transcends the meaning of his act: 'since I am what I am not and since I am not what I am – I can not even define myself as truly *being* in the process of listening at doors' (*BN*, p. 260). Even later on when he reflects upon his deed, he is not forced to identify himself with it. 'I am not really a voyeur', he might say to himself. 'What I did was simply an aberration. Besides, the me that I am now cannot be held responsible for past conduct. Already, I am no longer the person that I was.' However, if he is caught in the act, such reasoning – a classic example of bad faith – is far more difficult to indulge in, though not impossible. If he is caught in the act he is no longer entirely free to determine the meaning or lack of meaning of his act, for in a very real sense he is no longer in possession of its meaning. As a transcendence he escapes the meaning of his act. As a transcendence-transcended the meaning of his act escapes him and is lost to him. Suddenly, it belongs to the Other. The Other's possession of the meaning of his act is the negation of his capacity freely to interpret himself. His freedom is enslaved by the freedom of the Other.

> A judgement is the transcendental act of a free being. Thus being-seen constitutes me as a defenceless being for a freedom which is not my freedom. It is in this sense that we can consider ourselves 'slaves' . . . In so far as I am the object of values which come to qualify me without my being able to act on this qualification or even to know it, I am enslaved. (*BN*, p. 267)

A person's being-for-others is very much a being that he is, but he is it over there, for the Other, in so far as the Other is free to interpret and evaluate his actions as he sees fit. A person's being-for-others constitutes a whole range of (his) possibilities, but they are alienated possibilities. They are not possibilities that he maintains and controls through his own transcendence, but possibilities fixed by the transcendence of the Other.

> I grasp the Other's look at the very centre of my act as the solidification and alienation of my own possibilities. In fear or in anxious or prudent anticipation, I perceive that these possibilities which *I am* and which are the condition of my transcendence are given also to another, given as about to be transcended in turn by his own possibilities. (*BN*, p. 263)

Shame is one way in which being-for-others is revealed existentially. Alongside shame can be listed such related phenomena as guilt, embarrassment and paranoia. However, being-for-others is not limited to these unpleasant states of being. Being-for-others also accounts for pleasant states such as being proud or feeling flattered. Pleasure is gained here precisely because a person makes himself an object for the Other.[2] In making himself an object for the Other he enjoys relinquishing responsibility for his free transcendence: a responsibility that may well be a source of anguish. He may also take pleasure in reflecting on the pleasing object that he is for the Other.

In describing being-for-others it is important to note that the look does not permanently render a person an object for the Other. It is not the case that when the Other has transcended his transcendence he remains a transcendence permanently transcended. A person can also become Other for the Other by recovering his transcendence, thereby reducing the Other to an object. This is certainly the case in genuine interpersonal relationships where a person will find the opportunity to recover his transcendence. If the Other is at all well disposed towards him this recovery will be positively encouraged.[3]

Sartre characterizes interpersonal relations as a ceaseless, unresolvable power-struggle. Like Schopenhauer and Nietzsche before him, he is of the opinion that conflict is the essence of human relationships. Famously, he asserts in his play *No Exit* that 'Hell is other people' (*NE*, p. 127). Conflict may involve a struggle to dominate the transcendence of the Other and render it a transcendence transcended. This is the most familiar form of power-struggle. Alternatively, for masochists, it will involve conflict over who gets to be dominated.

Some critics resist Sartre's claim that the essence of all relationships is conflict, not because they think it is too pessimistic but simply because they think it is an unjustifiable generalization. Gregory McCulloch writes: 'What a sorry business this all is! Even though there is undoubtedly something that rings true in Sartre's account, we at least sometimes manage better than this . . . many of us seem often to rub along rather more harmoniously than Sartre would have it' (McCulloch 1994, p. 139). McCulloch goes on to suggest that to some degree Sartre's insistence on the universality of conflict is motivated by personal considerations. Sartre, he argues, is tempted to speak too much from his own experience and to play the novelist by overemphasizing one aspect of human nature. For her part, Marjorie Grene notes that Sartre seems to ignore the evidence of certain concrete situations when he suggests that the look is always threatening. She invites us to consider 'The rare but still indubitable experience of mutual understanding, of the reciprocal look of peers; or the look of mother and infant, where the one protects and the other is protected. In its immediate appearance there seems no internecine warfare here' (Grene 1983, p. 154). In his early philosophy at least, Sartre seems to lack an appreciation of the capacity people have for being with others – Heidegger's *Mitsein*. Here the self is not transcended by other people, nor does it seek to transcend other people. Rather, the self is transcended by some collective experience or enterprise in which the individual person becomes, or allows himself to become, submerged in an *us*. Of course, this submergence in an *us* is often maintained through conflict with a *them* as opponent and/or hate object – Sartrean conflict at the group level. However, there are occasions when the *us* does not require a *them* in order to be maintained. For example, a group may work together on a task with a common goal that is not primarily the goal of beating the competition. Alternatively, a group united together by religion, music, dancing or drugs may achieve a state of reverie amounting to a collective loss of self.

It is sometimes supposed that in identifying the phenomenon of being-for-others Sartre is claiming to have solved the problem of proving the existence of other minds; that he is claiming other minds must exist if a person can experience himself in the mode of being-for-others. Sartre, in fact, makes no such claim. Indeed, he holds that the problem of other minds is impossible to solve by any means. But even if he did not hold that the problem is impossible to solve, he would still readily agree that the problem cannot be solved via an appeal to the phenomenon of being-for-others. To feel shame, for example, a person need only believe that there is a mind behind a dis-approving look. He need not know there is a mind there, any more than a shoplifter need know that a security camera is working in order to feel he is being looked at. If, in order to experience shame, a person need only believe that he is seen by another person, then shame can arise when that belief is false. The existence of shame cannot remove the problem of other minds because it is possible that the belief in the Other that inspires shame might be a false belief on every occasion. On the grounds that the (supposed) for-itself of the Other is not on principle an object of knowledge the existence of which can be confirmed by experience, Sartre holds that the problem of other minds is impossible to solve by any means whatsoever. 'Since the Other on principle and in its "For-itself" is outside my experience, the probability of his existence as *another Self* can never be either validated or invalidated, it can be neither believed nor dis-believed, it can not even be measured; it loses therefore its very being as probability and becomes a pure fictional conjecture' (*BN*, p. 250).

Rather than seek to prove the existence of other minds, Sartre seeks to show that the existence of other minds cannot be realisti-cally doubted, given a person's own experience of himself as proud, embarrassed or ashamed before the Other. He holds that although the existence of the Other cannot be proven, it is continually sug-gested by intrinsic structures of a person's own being that cannot be described in terms of his being-in-the-world, but must be described in terms of his being-in-the-midst-of-the-world. Ironically, it is only when we seek to prove the existence of the Other that doubts about his existence creep in: 'if I do not conjecture about the Other, then, precisely I affirm him' (*BN*, p. 251).[4] Although the sceptic is correct in insisting that the existence of the Other cannot be proven, even the sceptic will find himself continually affirming the existence of the Other pre-reflectively in the way that he behaves and experiences his own being.

CHAPTER 3

THE BODY

The object which the things in the world indicate and which they include in their radius is for itself and on principle a non-object.

(*BN*, p. 318)

The human body is clearly fundamental to the human condition. An account of the human condition that does not consider the body is seriously incomplete. Sartre's distinction between being-for-itself and being-for-others provides the perfect basis for a consideration of the body because these two modes of being are the essential onto-logical features of the body, just as they are the essential ontological features of consciousness. At the heart of Sartre's view of the body is his recognition of a radical difference between the way a person's body exists for the person himself and the way it exists for other people.

> these two aspects of the body are on different and incommuni-cable levels of being, they can not be reduced to one another. Being-for-itself must be wholly body and it must be wholly consciousness; it can not be united with a body. Similarly being-for-others is wholly body; there are no 'psychic phenomena' there to be united with the body. There is nothing *behind* the body. But the body is wholly 'psychic'. We must now proceed to study these two modes of being which we find for the body. (*BN*, p. 305)

Human beings are objects. The body is an object amongst other objects affected by the same physical determinants that affect all objects. Heidegger refers to this as being-in-the-midst-of-the-world. This is a person's being considered from the point of view of others.

This, however, is only one of a person's modes of being; a mode of being logically subsequent to the mode of being Heidegger refers to as being-in-the-world. In this mode of being, which corresponds to being-for-itself, the body is not an object. Of course, to say that a person's body is not an object for him when he is in the mode of being-in-the-world, when he is that which transcends the world, is not to say that his body mysteriously ceases to be an object from the point of view of others. This would amount to the absurd claim that when he is in the mode of being-in-the-world his body becomes incorporeal. Nevertheless, the claim is that when he is in the mode of being-in-the-world his body is in a certain sense invisible to him, or, at least, that he is oblivious to his body as a thing. Although it happens to be the case that a person can see and touch his own body, it is not essential to his being-in-the-world that he can do so. It is possible to imagine a conscious creature that cannot see or touch its own body that spends its entire life oblivious to the fact that it has a body. 'It even appears that this is the case for certain insects which, although provided with a differentiated nervous system and with sense organs, can not employ this system and these organs to know each other' (*BN*, p. 358). There is no need to resort to the peculiar case of certain insects to illustrate the point. Wittgenstein, in his *Tractatus Logico-Philosophicus* illustrates the point using the human eye as an example: 'nothing *in the visual field* allows us to infer that it is seen by an eye' (Wittgenstein 2001, prop. 5.633). Although a person can see his eye in a mirror, the fact that the eye in the mirror is the very same eye that is seeing this reflection cannot be inferred directly from the eye in the mirror – the eye *in the visual field*. To infer that the eye in the mirror is the eye seeing its reflection a person must know certain facts about mirrors and the phenomenon of reflection. If a person had never encountered a mirror before he would mistake his reflection for another person. However, even when a person knows from experience that the eye in the mirror is the eye seeing the eye in the mirror, the eye in the mirror and the eye seeing the eye in the mirror remain ontologically distinct. The eye in the mirror, though he knows it is nobody's eye but his own, remains other. It is an object in the visual field. He sees it only as an object. He cannot and does not see the eye seeing. Making essentially the same point as Wittgenstein, Sartre imagines a situation in which a creature is physically constituted in such a way that one of its eyes can see the other eye:

nothing prevents me from imagining an arrangement of the sense organs such that a living being could see one of his eyes while the eye which was seen was directing its glance upon the world. But it is to be noted that in this case again I am the Other in relation to my eye. I apprehend it as a sense organ constituted in the world in a particular way, but I can not 'see the seeing'; that is, I can not apprehend it in the process of revealing an aspect of the world to me. Either it is a thing among other things, or else it is that by which other things are revealed to me. (*BN*, p. 304)

Both examples – an eye seeing itself in a mirror and one eye seeing the other eye directly – make the point that consciousness is not a psychic phenomenon magically attached to the body that can be observed deep within eyes in the form of a seen seeing. Rather, a person's body, as it is for the person himself, is wholly psychic; it *is* the for-itself. The body represents the immediate and inescapable situation of the for-itself that the for-itself perpetually surpasses towards future situations. The body is the contingent given which the for-itself perpetually transcends. Nonetheless, the for-itself is perpetually reapprehended by the body because the body is the very possibility, the very ground, of the transcendence of the for-itself. In other words, the for-itself is that which perpetually surpasses the body without ever being able to render the body finally and completely surpassed. 'The body is what I nihilate. It is the in-itself which is surpassed by the nihilating for-itself and which re-apprehends the for-itself in this very surpassing' (*BN*, p. 309). If the for-itself were able to surpass the body once and for all instead of being a perpetual surpassing of it, the for-itself would immediately cease to be. This is because the body is the immediate and ever-present situation of the for-itself. For the for-itself, to be and to be situated are one and the same. 'The body is not distinct from the *situation* of the for-itself since for the for-itself, to exist and to be situated are one and the same' (*BN*, p. 309). The body is the immediate and ever-present situation of the for-itself that the for-itself perpetually negates and surpasses. In existing as the surpassing negation of the body, the for-itself necessarily requires the body in order to realize itself as that which is nothing beyond the surpassing negation of the body.

Sartre's view of the body can be described in temporal terms: The for-itself, as a project towards the future, renders the body past (surpassed). The body, however, remains as an immediate past touching upon the present that the for-itself requires in order to launch itself towards the future. 'In each project of the for-itself, in each perception the body is there; it is the immediate Past in so far as it still touches on the Present which flees it' (*BN*, p. 326). The for-itself requires the body as the future requires the past.

What does the fact that the for-itself perpetually surpasses the body towards the future fulfilment of its projects imply about the instrumental status of the body? Sartre's explanation of the instrumental status of a person's body, as it is for the person himself, focuses on the example of a person absorbed in the task of writing. From the point of view of others, a person who is writing utilizes his hand as an instrument in order to utilize the pen as an instrument. For himself, however, he does not utilize his hand, he utilizes the pen in a hand that is himself. His hand is surpassed towards the project of writing and as such is not an object-hand. His hand is not acted upon by the for-itself; it is the for-itself acting in the world,

> I do not apprehend my hand in the act of writing but only the pen which is writing; this means that I use my pen in order to form letters but not my hand in order to hold the pen. I am not in relation to my hand in the same utilising attitude as I am in relation to the pen; *I am my hand*. The hand is only the utilisation of the pen. (*BN*, p. 323)

Following Heidegger, Sartre argues that the human world can be viewed as an infinity of potential systems of instrumentality. For a particular system of instrumentality to emerge from undifferentiated being – for it to become an actual system of instrumentality – there must be an 'arresting of references' (*BN*, p. 323) to which the entire system refers. Any system of instrumentality, in order for it to be a system of instrumentality, must refer back to that for which it is a system of instrumentality. In the case of the person who is writing, the hand is not an instrument in the system, but that to which an entire system of instrumentality refers. The system of instrumentality emerges by virtue of its orientation towards the hand in action: that is, the for-itself in action. The hand in action arrests the system, determines it, orientates it, gives it meaning, and so on. At the same time the system gives meaning to the activity of the hand.

the hand is at once the unknowable and non-utilisable term which the last instrument of the series indicates ('book to be read – characters to be formed on the paper – pen') and at the same time the orientation of the entire series (the printed book itself refers back to the hand). But I can apprehend it – at least in so far as it is acting – only as the perpetual, evanescent reference of the whole series. Thus in a duel with swords or with quarter-staffs, it is the quarter-staff which I watch with my eyes and which I handle. In the act of writing it is the point of the pen which I look at in synthetic combination with the line of the square marked on the sheet of paper. But my hand has vanished; it is lost in the complex system of instrumentality in order that this system may exist. It is simply the meaning and the orientation of the system. (*BN*, p. 323)

What Sartre says of the hand also applies to consciousness. A person's consciousness, which for others is amid the instrumentality of the world, is for the person himself the meaning and orientation of the system of instrumentality that he discloses through his purposeful activity.

Just as the for-itself surpasses the hand and makes it vanish as an object, so it can surpass the tool the hand is manipulating and make it vanish also. When a person has learnt to use a tool skilfully the tool is forgotten while in use; it is surpassed towards the task. It exists in the mode of what Heidegger refers to as ready-to-hand. The tool becomes an extension of the body as it acts towards its future goals: 'my body always extends across the tool which it utilizes: it is at the end of the cane on which I lean . . . it is at the end of the telescope which shows me the stars' (*BN*, p. 325). When a person pokes dirt with a stick in order to discover if it is soft or hard he feels the texture of the dirt there at the end of the stick, at which moment he does not feel the stick in his hand. Tools tend only to assert their independence from a person and remind him of their existence when they fail, or when he fails to manipulate them correctly. That is, when they suddenly cease to be an instrument for him and instead present themselves as an obstacle. Here they present themselves in the mode of what Heidegger refers to as being present-at-hand. For example, I only pay attention to the instrumental system with which I am typing these words when, as a result of malfunction or user error, it presents itself as obstinate. When both it and I are functioning correctly I forget it as I forget my own body. When the whole ensemble is running smoothly, I give no thought to my hands, to the keyboard, even to the screen at which I gaze. They all cease to be objects for me and become instead the transcended, surpassed moments of my overall project of writing.[1]

A person's body is his consciousness, in the sense that he is not in the world as a passive awareness but as a being that acts towards the future. It can be said that his body is absorbed by his consciousness, although this form of words tends to suggest that consciousness and body are two distinct phenomena that could exist separately but happen to be united. To say that consciousness is embodied is not to say that consciousness happens to ride around inside the body, but that embodiment is consciousness's way of being-in-the-world, and its only way. The existence of each and every embodied person is contingent, but given that a person exists, it is absolutely necessary that he be embodied. 'It [my body] is therefore in no way a contingent addition to my soul; on the contrary it is a permanent structure of my being and the permanent condition of possibility for my consciousness as consciousness of the world and as a transcendent project toward my future' (*BN*, p. 328).

Sartre's existentialism rules out disembodied consciousnesses and disembodied souls. It contains no notion of an afterlife and is profoundly atheistic and anti-metaphysical. The for-itself is transcendent, but not in a metaphysical sense. It is transcendent only in so far as it is the temporal transcendence of the immediate in-itself of the body and the particular situation of the body. The transcendence that is the for-itself is the transcendence of the body. No body, no transcendence. No transcendence, no for-itself.

Further to this account of Sartre's view of the body I will now consider two criticisms that have been levelled against it. These criticisms centre on the claim that Sartre draws too sharp a distinction between the body as it is for the self and the body as it is for others. It is argued that in drawing such a sharp distinction, Sartre misrepresents a person's relationship with his own body and underestimates the importance of embodiment in the experience of others as subjects.

Regarding the first criticism, it is claimed that Sartre misrepresents a person's relationship with his own body by insisting that the person is oblivious to his own body when he is in the transcendent mode of being. Recall Sartre's example of the spy at the keyhole. According to Sartre, while the spy is absorbed in his task he is a pure consciousness of things. It is only when the spy believes he is seen that he becomes aware of his body. This is in keeping with Sartre's general position that a person's embodied self is disclosed to him through others. 'The unreflective consciousness does not apprehend the person [its own embodied self] directly or as its object; the person is presented to consciousness in so far as the person is an object for the Other' (*BN*, p. 260). Disagreeing with Sartre, some critics have argued that it is not only via others that a person apprehends his embodied self but that there is also non-thetic consciousness of embodiment that does not require others. Sartre implicitly denies non-thetic consciousness of embodiment when he writes: 'I am for myself only as I am a pure reference to the Other' (*BN*, p. 260). Yet, as Sartre's critics point out, the presence of non-thetic consciousness of embodiment is strongly suggested by his own example of the spy. Before the spy becomes ashamed he is jealous. In being jealous the spy is not, according to Sartre, aware of his body, because jealousy, unlike shame, is not jealousy before someone. A person is jealous of others, not jealous before others. Sartre's critics agree with him that jealousy is not jealousy before someone. They do not agree, however, that prior to the advent of his shame, while he is only jealous, the spy is oblivious to his body. Even though jealousy is not before someone, it discloses a person's body to him as much as shame does. Just as when a person is ashamed he experiences himself as having a hot face, sweaty palms and a pounding heart, when he is jealously spying on his unfaithful wife he experiences himself as having a stealthy posture, bated breath and a knotted feeling in his stomach. The general point is that regardless of whether or not emotional states are before someone, all emotional states disclose the embodied self. So long as a person is not unconscious his body is always disclosed to him one way or another because every conscious experience has its accompanying bodily state of which the person is immediately and pre-reflectively aware. Kathleen Wider even argues in *The Bodily Nature of Consciousness* that pre-reflective bodily awareness is the very basis of consciousness. Recall Sartre's view that without non-thetic self-consciousness the for-itself cannot be conscious because to be conscious is to be conscious of being so. For Wider, this non-thetic self-consciousness is fundamentally bodily awareness; what she calls bodily self-consciousness. Consciousness, she argues, is rooted in the presence of the body to itself as presence to the world: 'the body must be present to itself in being present to the world.

So there must be a kind of consciousness of the body, what I will call bodily self-consciousness, and this must form part of our awareness of the world. The most basic form of self-consciousness must be bodily awareness' (Wider 1997, p. 115).

The second criticism, that Sartre underestimates the importance of embodiment in the experience of the Other as a subject, is raised by his contemporary Maurice Merleau-Ponty in *Phenomenology of Perception*. As seen, Sartre supposes that the Other must exist for me, as I must exist for the Other, as either transcendent subject or transcended object. The Other exists for me as a subject only when he transcends my transcendence and reduces me to an object. The problem with this picture is that it ignores the fact that the Other exists for me most frequently as an embodied consciousness. That is, I am most often aware of the Other as a subject, not because my experience of my own embodiment indicates a subject who has transcended me, but because I experience a living, acting, embodied subject before me; a subject incarnate. I do not experience him either as an Other or as a body; his Otherness and his embodiment are given together. To be conscious of the Other as angry, for example, is not simply to be conscious that he poses a threat to my body, it is to be conscious of him as embodying anger. Of course, in so far as his anger is inspired by and directed towards something external to his body, his anger is not reducible to his bodily state, but this is not to say that his bodily state merely indicates his anger. There is a very real sense in which his clenched fists and his rolling eyeballs are his anger. If I am witness to these bodily states then I am witness to his anger, not to the outward signs of an anger taking place in the privacy of his subjectivity. Sartre acknowledges as much when he writes:

> These frowns, this redness, this stammering, this slight trembling of the hands, these downcast looks which seem at once timid and threatening – these do not express anger; they are the anger. But this point must be clearly understood. In itself a clenched fist is nothing and means nothing. But also we never perceive a clenched fist. We perceive a man who in a certain situation clenches his fist. (*BN*, pp. 346–7)

Unfortunately, Sartre does not allow such a valuable insight into the meaning and significance of embodied consciousness to sway him from his questionable view that a person's experience of another person as a subject always involves him experiencing himself as an object for the other person. Sartre insists on treating what is just one possible way of experiencing others – as a threat – as though it were the only way people can experience one another as subjects.

PART 2

FREEDOM

CHAPTER 4

EXISTENTIAL FREEDOM

Man can not be sometimes slave and sometimes free; he is wholly and forever free or he is not free at all.

(*BN*, p. 441)

Sartre's theory of freedom emerges out of a dissatisfaction with the traditional debate – a debate he refers to as 'those tedious discussions between determinists and the proponents of free will' (*BN*, p. 436). The traditional debate consists of a series of arguments that claim in their various ways that free will is an illusion and that everything that happens, including everything that people do, is causally or logically necessitated. Each argument for determinism or pre-determinism is followed by its accompanying refutation in favour of free will. By this process the free will that people naturally assume they have is defended against the perceived threat of determinism. Unfortunately, the traditional debate says very little about free will except that there are apparently no indubitable reasons to suppose that people do not possess it. It seeks to make room for free will but it does not say how free will is possible or what it really involves. Within the traditional debate, free will remains a mysterious capacity. The theory of freedom offered by existential phenomenology on the other hand attempts to demystify free will by showing that it is an intrinsic and necessary feature of the human condition: a feature that is directly implied by the very nature of consciousness as being-for-itself. Although free will is a contingent fact – because being-for-itself is a contingent fact – given that there is being-for-itself, it is necessary that this being be free. Furthermore, as will be seen, the account of human free will offered by existential phenomenology also offers valuable insights into human psychology and behaviour.

Although the traditional debate has tended to proceed by way of hard determinists and 'free will partisans' (*BN*, p. 490) placing themselves at loggerheads with one another, more subtle thinkers have recognized the need to reach a compromise and develop theories showing that free will and determinism are compatible. As a result, the theories of soft determinism and compatibilism have emerged. If free will and determinism are utterly incompatible and free will is simply freedom from all constraint, then free will cannot be determined in any way. Only random, chaotic behaviour in an equally random and chaotic world could count as an expression of free will. But acting freely is not acting in a random and chaotic manner. It is acting with reason and purpose in a world that is structured and predictable to a significant degree. If chaos reigned and there was no way of establishing imperatives of the form 'If you want *x* then do *y*', then meaningful action would be impossible and, hence, the possibility of acting freely. Without a reasonably coherent framework of conditions within which to act the only possibility would be to act like the proverbial headless chicken. Freedom is not free fall and free action requires that a person act within a situation that has a degree of coherence. As will be seen, in the view of existential phenomenology, free will and determinism are not only compatible, they necessarily require one another. They are the internally related aspects of an original synthesis.

THE NECESSITY OF FREEDOM

The respective arguments for free will and determinism generate an apparently insoluble dilemma. On the one hand, there seems to be no denying that everything is determined by universal causality, while on the other hand, the human condition seems incomprehensible if it is denied that people are self-determined and responsible beings capable of choice. That is, it seems impossible to understand people other than as beings who somehow transcend the causal order. In a totally determined universe there could be no possibilities or alternatives. Hence, there could be no minds because the essence of minds is to raise possibilities and conceive of alternatives. A philosopher confronted with the dilemma of free will and determinism and the need to respect at least some of the claims of both determinists and free will advocates has several options. The worst of these is to conclude that free will and determinism must be compatible, but only God knows how. This is Descartes' approach. As Leibniz says of him:

> That distinguished philosopher . . . could not unravel these knots . . . but preferred to cut them with a sword. For he says we can easily involve ourselves in great difficulties if we try to reconcile God's preordination with the freedom of the will, and that we must abstain from discussing them, since God's nature can not be comprehended by us. (Leibniz 1990b, p. 107)

Although Leibniz makes some advance on the Cartesian mysticism or defeatism that he criticizes, his own attempts to reconcile freedom and determinism are also unsatisfactory. According to Leibniz, God's omniscience ensures that God knows exactly what a person will do in future. For God, a person cannot do otherwise and is therefore not free. Nevertheless, according to Leibniz, a person is free within the bounds of his own limited perspective because he does not know what he will do in future. His finite understanding means that he is unaware of what God knows he will do and so he is able at least to conceive of alternatives, even if he is not able to take them. However, alternatives that can be conceived of but not actually taken without defying God's omniscience are not genuine alternatives. There is a crucial difference between genuine alternatives that a person could have taken, and merely apparent alternatives that he could not in fact have taken. The freedom Leibniz argues for amounts only to an appearance of freedom. Leibniz's whole position is clouded by his insistence on developing an ontology from the starting-point of a Supreme Being. His efforts are directed at salvaging human free will from beneath the steamroller of God's omniscience rather than at providing a genuine account of it.

What is required is an ontology that accounts for free will, not one that simply allows room for it. Such an ontology must be able to embrace the strongest arguments for both free will and determinism by reconciling these arguments. Not least, it must be capable of acknowledging and absorbing paradoxes rather than resisting them as problematic notions indicative of confusion and absurdity. I aim to show that existential phenomenology is uniquely capable of meeting these demands. Its account of freedom follows directly from the phenomenological account of the paradoxical nature of consciousness provided earlier in this book.

Descartes is unable to reconcile free will and determinism because he knows only of external relations. Sartre, however, has at his disposal the Hegelian concept of the internal relation or internal negation. It is the concept of the internal relation, in which two apparently irreconcilable terms each have their meaning in and through the other, that is central to Sartre's solution to the dilemma or paradox of free will and determinism.

In Sartre's view, there is an internal relation existing between what is free and what is transcended by freedom and is not free. This internal relation is best understood, at least initially, in terms of the internal relation existing between past and future. Certainly, it is Sartre's view of temporality, his view of the for-itself as essentially temporal, which renders plausible his view of the for-itself as necessarily free. He argues that 'Human reality is a perpetual surpassing towards a coincidence with itself which is never given' (*BN*, p. 89). Unlike being-in-itself, the for-itself is never identical with itself, but always beyond itself towards the future. It exists not as a present immanence but as that which is its own future. That each person is a being towards the future is a claim that remains central to Sartre's thought, even in such a relatively unrepresentative work as *Existentialism and Humanism.*[1] As he says in that otherwise largely rejected essay: 'man is, before all else, something which propels itself towards a future and is aware that it is doing so' (*EAH*, p. 28).

The present is the presence of the for-itself to the in-itself. The for-itself is nothing in itself; it is nothing in the present. As such, it stands outside the causal order. The causal order, that which is, that which cannot be other than it is once it has come to pass, belongs to a past which the for-itself realizes by constituting itself as the future of that past. Although the meaning of the past can change, the past is determined in so far as it is that being which has been given. However, the past is given to the for-itself in terms of the future possibilities that the for-itself realizes for this given being. Indeed, the for-itself consists entirely of these possibilities. The for-itself is the possibilities of being: possibilities that being cannot realize for itself, but which must be realized for it from the point of view of its negation. The for-itself requires a given being in order to be that which temporally transcends it towards the future: to be that which renders it past as it transcends. There is no past except for that which is a being towards the future and no being towards the future except as a surpassing. Future and past are internally related, they necessarily require one another.

As nothing but a being towards the future, as nothing but the future possibilities of the being of which it is the negation, the for-itself has to be these possibilities. It cannot not be an opening up of possibilities. The freedom of the for-itself consists in this perpetual opening up of the possibilities of being. That is, the for-itself perpetually discovers itself in a world of possibilities which it realizes by virtue of its being a temporal surpassing towards the future. If it were not a surpassing, it would not find itself in a world of possibilities but rather in a strictly determined world. Of course, as it is nothing but the temporal surpassing of that which has been given it could not exist in such a world.

That which is free – the for-itself as a being towards the future – and that which is not free – the in-itself that the for-itself renders past by surpassing it towards the future – are internally related in that the for-itself necessarily requires the in-itself in order to be a free surpassing. (This is the internal relation of facticity and transcendence and will be considered shortly.) Moreover, it is necessary that the for-itself be a free surpassing of being if it is to be at all. This is the necessity of freedom. The being of the for-itself is contingent, but given that it exists, it is absolutely necessary that it be free. The for-itself is essentially free and it is a necessary condition of its existence that it is not free to cease being free.

The for-itself can never surrender its freedom. It can never render itself an object causally determined by the physical world, for the very project of surrender, the very attempt to render itself causally determined, must be a free choice of itself. The for-itself cannot render itself determined by the world, for whenever or however it attempts to do so, it must choose to do so. 'Not to choose is, in fact, to choose not to choose' (BN, p. 481). An absolute necessity, an absolute determinant, lies at the very heart of the freedom of the for-itself. The for-itself cannot not choose; it cannot not be free. 'Freedom is the freedom of choosing but not the freedom of not choosing' (BN, p. 481). The for-itself does not choose itself as a freedom, it is necessarily free. It is condemned to be free by virtue of its existence as a non-being that must be its own nothingness. 'I am condemned to exist forever beyond my essence, beyond the causes and motives of my act. I am condemned to be free. This means that no limit to my freedom can be found except freedom itself or, if you prefer, that we are not free to cease being free' (BN, p. 439).

The traditional debate is fundamentally misguided in aiming to dismiss completely either free will or determinism. What must be understood is that what is free and what is not free are internally related; the former is dependent on the latter and finds its meaning and possibility in and through the latter. That is, the for-itself, as freedom and as consciousness of freedom, must be a free surpassing negation of the given situation. It must perpetually transcend what Sartre calls facticity in order to exist. Facticity is 'The coefficient of adversity of things' (*BN*, p. 481). Facticity is the world around a person in so far as it presents a constant resistance to his actions and projects – difficulties, obstacles, entanglements, snags, distances, heaviness, instability, fragility, complexity, and so on. Yet this constant resistance is the very possibility of a person's actions in that his actions are always a striving to overcome facticity. As Simone de Beauvoir writes: 'The resistance of the thing sustains the action of man as air sustains the flight of the dove' (de Beauvoir 2000, p. 81). It is only as a free surpassing negation of facticity that the for-itself has being. If there were no facticity to be surpassed and overcome there would be no for-itself. As a free transcendence towards its own future the for-itself necessarily requires something to transcend. The for-itself is, so to speak, perpetually striving to escape from the prison of facticity without ever being able to do so. For the for-itself, to be escaping and to be are one and the same.

The freedom of the for-itself consists in a transcendent flight towards an open future away from the facticity of a present revealed as past by the very flight of the for-itself. In order to realize the chosen future towards which it strives, in order to obtain its future, the for-itself must realize it, must obtain it, as past. Reaching the future renders the future past, renders it facticity for a further transcendence. 'The future does not allow itself to be rejoined; it slides into the Past as a bygone future, and the Present for-itself in all its facticity is revealed as the foundation of its own nothingness and once again as the lack of a new future' (*BN*, p. 128). The future is never realized other than as a past-future; as future it is nothing but a future-past. The for-itself is free because it is a perpetual passing beyond and negation of its facticity and its past which would determine it if it were identical with itself. For Sartre, 'facticity' and 'past' indicate one and the same phenomena. A person is his facticity, his past, but always as a surpassing: 'The past is the in-itself which I am, but I am this in-itself as *surpassed*' (*BN*, p. 118).

That the future can never be realized as future implies that the future is for-itself and not in-itself. It is because determinists view the future as in-itself, as an already existing being to be arrived at, that they believe the future is determined. However, viewed as nothing but the being beyond itself of the for-itself and nothing but the possibilities towards which the for-itself projects itself, the future is recognized as being truly open and indeterminate. That the future will be something or other does not mean that a particular future is waiting in the wings: 'We must not understand by the future a "now" which is not yet' (*BN*, p. 125). Neither should the future be understood as an infinite set of alternative nows, some of which will be encountered, some of which will not. This is still to view the future as though it were in-itself. Neither is the future a mere representation on the part of the for-itself: 'We must abandon from the start the idea that the future exists as representation' (*BN*, p. 124). In contemplating what the future might be a person is not contemplating his future. For a person to imagine what may happen to him in future is not for him to foresee what will happen. Genuine contemplation of his future would require his future to be the present content of his representation. If the future were such a representation in the present then the for-itself would be limited to the present. Representation could aim only at the present and not at the future.

Although representation aims at the future it is only an expected future that can be represented, not an actual one. The future has no actuality. Rather than being a representation, a person's future is ' "I" in as much as I await myself as presence to a being beyond being' (*BN*, p. 127). The future is the for-itself in so far as the for-itself is that which must exist beyond itself as a perpetually indeterminate being. The future is what the for-itself lacks; the for-itself is this lack. The for-itself is free because the future, far from being that which places external constraints upon the free transcendence of the for-itself, is the for-itself as that which the for-itself is not yet.

> The future is revealed to the for-itself as that which the for-itself is not yet, inasmuch as the for-itself constitutes itself non-thetically for itself as a not-yet in the perspective of this revelation, and inasmuch as it makes itself be as a project of itself outside the present towards that which is not yet. (*BN*, p. 126)

The internal relationship between freedom and facticity is at one with the internal relationship between consciousness and the world. Freedom is not a capacity of consciousness; freedom is of the very nature of consciousness. Freedom is not an essence, just as consciousness is not an essence. It is not a potential that exists prior to being exercised. Freedom is its exercise. Understanding action and choice, therefore, is the key to understanding Sartre's theory of freedom.

ACTION, CHOICE AND THE INDETERMINACY OF THE SELF

The defining characteristic of an action, as distinct from a mere accidental act, is intention. An intention, a chosen end to be realized in the future, gives meaning to the present actions that aim at it and are a means to it. When intentions are realized and ends achieved, however, they themselves immediately become means to further ends, with no achieved end ever able fully and finally to satisfy, define and determine the for-itself. The for-itself, as a being that must be a perpetual flight towards the future, must always surpass whatever chosen ends it realizes for itself towards further chosen ends. Each word I write here, for example, is surpassed by the sentence, each sentence by the page, each page by the book, and so on, with each larger chosen end giving meaning to the complex of actions that serve it. Ultimately, the myriad projects of the for-itself aim at making the for-itself a for-itself-in-itself; they aim at realizing an unachievable state of fulfilment and completion in which the for-itself is a being at one with itself rather than a non-being. Sartre, as noted, argues that the fundamental project of the for-itself is to be God.

Each for-itself aims to be a for-itself-in-itself in its own way. The particular fulfilment and completion at which an individual for-itself aims depends upon its own particular fundamental choice of itself.[2] Fundamental choice is a choice of self that aims to establish an individual for-itself as a being that is no longer in question. However, as the fundamental choice must be continually affirmed or denied, or possibly abandoned for an alternative fundamental choice, it does not serve to place the being of the for-itself beyond question. It remains the case that the nature of the for-itself is to have no nature other than to be a perpetual questioning of its nature. As Simone de Beauvoir argues throughout *The Ethics of Ambiguity*, man's nature or essence is to have no nature or essence. Greater sense can be made of this claim by considering, for example, the nature of cowardice.

The man who chooses to believe or even simply to suspect that he is a coward is likely to live his life seeking to refute this belief. He may perform many acts of bravery with the intention of overcoming his suspicion. He may even become a hero in the opinion of others. Yet, for himself, he will remain unable to be at one with the label 'brave'. However many acts of bravery he performs, once performed these acts will become part of his past. Contemplating the future he can say, and will say so long as his fundamental choice of himself is as a coward, 'It seems I was brave, but will I continue to be so? In future battles I fear I will reveal myself to be a coward. I fear I will run away; it is certainly possible.' Equally, he is unable to be at one with the label 'coward' should he try to accept himself as a coward. In attempting to accept himself as a coward doubts would inevitably creep in. It might occur to him that accepting himself as a coward is a brave thing to do if he must brave the shame of being a coward. Future circumstances might also throw his cowardice into doubt. Suppose a bully picks once too often on a man who has always considered himself to be a coward and has always acted accordingly. Suppose the bully finally makes the man so angry that before he has had time to reflect upon his belief in himself as a coward he beats the bully unconscious. Following such an incident, the man might conclude that his anger temporarily overcame his enduring cowardice. Alternatively, he might conclude that he is not really a coward after all and has been mistaken all his life to consider himself as one. The indeterminacy of the self as revealed through the example of cowardice is well summed up in the following passage:

> One of the charges most often laid against the *Chemins de la Liberté* is something like this – 'But, after all, these people being so base, how can you make them into heroes?' The objection is really rather comic, for it implies that people are born heroes: and that is, at bottom, what such people would like to think. If you are born cowards, you can be quite content, you can do nothing about it and you will be cowards all your lives whatever you do; and if you are born heroes you can again be quite content; you will be heroes all your lives, eating and drinking heroically. Whereas the existentialist says that the coward makes himself cowardly, the hero makes himself heroic; and that there is always

a possibility for the coward to give up cowardice and for the hero to stop being a hero. (*EAH*, p. 43)

The ever-present possibility of transcending a label in the future necessarily prevents a person from ever permanently attaching a label to himself. To attach a label permanently is, in fact, to have to re-attach it permanently; a necessary condition of the possibility of reattachment being that the person may choose not to reattach it. Until death, a person can never arrive at a position where redefinition is impossible; a position where he is at one with himself with the threat or promise of redefining factors excluded. A person is what he has decided to be, but he cannot really *be* it because it is always possible to decide otherwise. Past decisions and past resolutions can always be overturned.

Consider another example. Yesterday, a man decided he would give up smoking. He redefined himself as a non-smoker. Today he finds there is nothing to bind him to his decision. Certainly not his determination to quit smoking, for determination can only ever be based upon a free choice to be determined. Even his doctor's warning that he will die if he continues cannot help him, for he must not only choose to take his doctor's advice into account, he must choose to follow it. If he starts to smoke again it does not even necessarily signify that he has dismissed his doctor's advice, for he may respect his doctor's opinion. Rather, it is the case that he is free to ignore good advice even in face of death. Good advice, in itself, has no causal efficacy. Advice may motivate action, but a motive is not an efficient cause.

What, then, can be said of people who have never smoked – people who never give the possibility of smoking a serious thought? Surely, they do not perpetually choose themselves as smoker or non-smoker? To answer this question the existentialist view of lack must be recalled. When the for-itself chooses a particular course of action it must choose it in terms of a perceived lack: 'the action necessarily implies as its condition the recognition of a "desideratum"; that is, of an objective lack or again of a *négatité* [negativity]' (*BN*, p. 433). The person who has never smoked and never thinks about the possibility of smoking, as opposed to the smoker who wants to quit or the quitter who wants to resume, does not perceive lacks with regard to smoking (i.e., the lack of a nicotine hit or the lack of good health). Rather, he will be concerned with realizing himself through the overcoming of other lacks that have nothing whatsoever to do with smoking or not smoking.

These remarks regarding lack suggest that once a person has been a smoker he will always be a smoker: either a smoker who smokes at present or a smoker who does not smoke at present. Arguably, even a person who has quit smoking (so far) continues to be defined in terms of the lack of a cigarette in a way that a person who has never smoked is not defined. For a one-time smoker, lack of tobacco is an existential lack. Tobacco is absent from his life in a way comparable to the absence of an expected friend. As for the true non-smoker, lack of tobacco is a purely abstract lack. Tobacco is absent from his life in a way comparable to the absence of a stranger who is not expected. (Recall Sartre's café example, considered earlier, in which he compares the existential absence of an expected friend with the abstract absence of Wellington [BN, pp. 9–10].) True, tobacco is not present in the life of the non-smoker, but neither is it missing.

To judge the strength of these claims individual cases must be considered. It depends how deeply rooted a person's choice of himself as a smoker is; the extent to which he chooses himself as a certain kind of lack to be overcome by smoking. Fortunately, for people who want to break the smoking habit, it is conceivable that in time a one-time smoker could entirely cease to choose himself as a certain kind of lack to be overcome by smoking, by redefining himself in terms of other lacks that have nothing to do with smoking.

To draw from this consideration of smokers and non-smokers what is most relevant to the purpose of outlining the view that the self is essentially indeterminate, consider the comically irresolute person who can neither accept himself as a smoker nor as a true non-smoker – a smoker who, for example, also chooses himself as another kind of lack to be overcome by good health. One day he will smoke and worry about his health; the next he will take exercise and find himself looking forward to a cigarette at the end of his workout. This predicament will not be due to devil-like desires struggling within him, or even to shame at the weakness of his will, but to a distressing inability that results directly from his freedom to stick to whichever choice he makes. He is unable to stick to whichever choice he makes because he is unable to exercise choice in order to limit, once and for all, his freedom to choose. As noted, the for-itself cannot not be free.

The claim that the for-itself cannot not be free sheds light on the nature of commitment. That the for-itself cannot escape the necessity of choice implies that commitment is not grounded upon itself. Indeed, commitment is nothing in itself. Rather, it consists entirely in the constant reaffirmation of a certain choice set against the ever-present lurking possibility of a change of mind. Herein, for example, lies the lover's dilemma. The beloved would have it that their lover's love be given freely, for love that is purchased is not love. Yet at the same time, because the beloved's happiness depends upon the precarious love of their lover (a thought which makes them insecure and not as happy as they expect to be) they want the love of their lover to be a determinate, assured thing – a love-in-itself. However, a love that could not not be given, a love that was not the result of a free choice to love but was simply there, would be worthless and would not be love. Incidentally, these remarks help to explain why the beloved may feel inclined to mistreat the lover. A love that is continually encouraged with kindness, gifts and flattery may begin to appear to the one indulging in this encouragement to be a love that is purchased rather than a love that is freely given. Rather than continue to encourage the love of their lover, the beloved may be tempted to test it for authenticity with bad behaviour. Seemingly, although people value a love that is won at high price, they do not always value a love that is maintained at high price. Sometimes people only value things that cost them nothing.

People are defined by what they lack. A person who has recently quit smoking, for example, is tense and irritable because he is engaged in a world that is bleak for him because it lacks tobacco. Lack, however, does more than simply determine a person's psychological state. A person makes sense of himself and his world in terms of what he perceives to be presently lacking.

A for-itself always perceives its situation as lacking something. However, as situations do not lack anything in themselves, whatever the situation of a for-itself lacks must, in fact, be a lack for that for-itself. In short, a for-itself introduces lack into its situation. What a situation lacks constitutes the possibilities of that situation. Therefore, the possibilities of a situation – by virtue of which it is a situation – are really nothing but the possibilities of a for-itself in that situation. A situation is never its own situation, it is always a situation for and the situation of a for-itself. The nature, meaning and value that a situation has is bestowed upon it by a for-itself for which it is a situation. Sartre illustrates this point with the following example:

> A particular crag, which manifests a profound resistance if I wish to displace it, will be on the contrary a valuable aid if I want to climb upon it in order to look over the countryside. In itself – if one can even imagine what the crag can be in itself – it is neutral; that is, it waits to be illuminated by an end in order to manifest itself as adverse or helpful. (*BN*, p. 482)

The nature, meaning and value of a crag depends upon the ends of the person who encounters it. If the projected end of the person is to climb the crag then it will manifest itself in the situation of that person as climbable or unclimbable, difficult to climb or easy to climb, and so on. The exact detail of the manifestation will depend on further factors relating to the person: how determined they are; how fit they are; their skill as a climber; the tools they have at their disposal, etc. 'Again it can manifest itself in one or the other way only within an instrumental-complex which is already established' (*BN*, p. 482). The way in which these factors affect the situation depends in large part upon previous choices that a person has made. Their skill as a climber will mainly be a result of past decisions to learn the art. Their overall determination in the past and at present in face of the crag will reveal their choice of themselves as a trier or as a 'sissy' (*BN*, p. 455).[3] On the other hand, the person who has no intention of climbing the crag will, if he notices the crag at all, view it only as an aesthetic object that he finds pleasing or displeasing according to his taste.

Finally, by way of further supporting Sartre's claim that the for-itself cannot not be free, it is worth noting that choosing a particular course of action always involves not choosing another course of action that could have been chosen. Unless a person has, for example, been reduced to a projectile by falling off a cliff, there are always alternative courses of action that he can take. When people say, for example, 'I have no choice but to act as I do', they ignore the fact that they can choose to do nothing. This is not to suggest that inaction is always a sensible option, merely that it is always a possible option. If someone says they will kill a man's family if he does not cooperate, he is not thereby causally determined to cooperate. He can still choose not to. A decision to cooperate is still his choice.[4]

Similarly, when people say, 'I can do nothing', they ignore the fact that they can always choose to do something, even if all they can do for the time being is plan how they might escape from their real or metaphorical chains.

THE LIMITS OF FREEDOM – CRITICISMS OF SARTRE'S THEORY OF FREEDOM

There are three good reasons for considering criticisms of Sartre's theory of freedom. First, addressing criticisms helps to clarify the theory. Second, as the best-known area of Sartre's existentialism, his theory of freedom is the area most commonly misrepresented by popular accounts that oversimplify key concepts and disrespect precise meanings. There is a greater need here than elsewhere, therefore, to defend Sartre against a number of unfounded criticisms based only on confusion that seek to make a mockery of his thought. Third, there are some criticisms of his theory of freedom that are at least tenable and at most identify genuine problems.

Sartre has sometimes been accused of treating freedom as an abstract, formal essence: as an in-itself that is identical in all contexts. This criticism is unfounded. It supposes that Sartre begins with an abstract notion of freedom that he then applies in all contexts, when in fact his method is to identify what is common across the whole diverse range of individual free projects. What is common across the range is that every free project, regardless of its situation, is a free surpassing negation of being towards the future. That a general feature of freedom is notable across the range of human experience does not indicate the presence of a universal human nature, but rather the presence of a universality of condition. Sartre consistently denies the existence of human nature as supposedly indicated by the universality of human freedom and is concerned that his references to a human condition are not taken as references to human nature.

> although it is impossible to find in each and every man a universal essence that can be called human nature, there is nevertheless a human universality of *condition*. (*EAH*, p. 45–6)

> What men have in common is not a 'nature' but a condition, that is, an ensemble of limits and restrictions: the inevitability of

death, the necessity of working for a living, of living in a world already inhabited by other men. Fundamentally this condition is nothing more than the basic human situation, or, if you prefer, the ensemble of abstract characteristics common to all situations. (*AJ*, p. 60)

Whatever the context, every for-itself is a non-being in relation to being and a free striving project towards the future. This expresses the universal condition of the for-itself in the abstract. As the for-itself does not exist in the abstract, however, it is vital to add that the context of each for-itself, and therefore the project of each for-itself, is wholly unique. Incidentally, it is no objection to the claim that each person is wholly unique to insist on the fact that people often have similar backgrounds, similar lives and similar aspirations. To be similar is not to be identical. Twins who have experienced the same environment from birth are still two different points of view on the world. Experiencing the same environment does not make their experiences identical; it does not make them identical people: 'Valéry is a petit bourgeois intellectual, but not every petit bourgeois intellectual is Valéry' (*POM*, p. 56).

Another unfounded criticism of Sartre's theory of freedom is that he treats freedom as unlimited when he should recognize that freedom is limited in the sense that each for-itself exercises its freedom in response to a necessarily finite range of options. It is argued, for example, that the freedom of St Paul was limited by his historical and geographical situation. He was free to convert to Christianity, an available option, but was not free to convert to Buddhism, which he had never heard of. Dismissing this objection, Sartre would insist that he is fully aware St Paul was not free to convert to Buddhism; although saying he was 'not free' is a misleading way of making the point. Not having the option of becoming a Buddhist did not present a limitation to St Paul's freedom; just as I cannot be said to be more free than Captain Cook because I have the option of flying to Australia. Sartre does not claim that the for-itself is limitlessly free in the sense that it confronts a limitless range of options. Rather, the for-itself is limitlessly free in the sense that it can never not choose itself through its choice of response to a particular situation. Although the options in any situation are limited, there is no limit to the responsibility of having to choose an option in every situation. 'What is not possible is not to choose. I can always choose, but I must know that if

I do not choose, that is still a choice' (*EAH*, p. 48). Critics who misunderstand Sartre to the point of insulting his intelligence argue, for example, that a person with no legs is not free to walk. This, of course, is true if freedom is equated with ability. Sartre, however, does not equate freedom with ability. A person with no legs is not able to walk, but this does not make him any less free according to Sartre's definition of freedom. For Sartre, freedom is limitless because a person must always choose himself in response to the facticity of his situation. With regard to the disabled person, he must choose the meaning of his disability. That he cannot choose himself as a footballer because he is disabled does not mean that he does not have to choose himself as something else. If he considers himself utterly ruined because he cannot choose himself as a footballer, that is his choice for which he alone is responsible. '. . . I can not be crippled without choosing myself as crippled. This means that I choose the way in which I constitute my disability' (*BN*, p. 328). Existentialism is certainly an uncompromising philosophy, which is no argument against it unless its uncompromising stance leads to philosophical error.

So far I have merely defended Sartre's thesis that freedom is limitless against criticisms based on misunderstanding. However, there are other more cogent criticisms of this thesis arguing that it is too uncompromising to provide an adequate account of the complexities of human behaviour. I will consider these criticisms in due course when I look at the more serious attacks that have been made on Sartre's theory of freedom.

The best-known criticisms of Sartre's theory of freedom are those made by his contemporary Maurice Merleau-Ponty in *Phenomenology of Perception*, a book largely conceived as a response to *Being and Nothingness*. In Merleau-Ponty's view, the failure of Sartre's early philosophy to acknowledge the importance of history upon the development of consciousness is a serious oversight resulting in the partial misrepresentation of several core existentialist concepts. In particular, freedom is reduced to an individual 'intellectual project' (Merleau-Ponty 2002, p. 447). The future is characterized as the outcome of a conscious decision that is chosen as though it were something already envisaged. Although this describes the everyday projects of a person who, for example, chooses to walk in the park because he envisages doing so as a way of overcoming his lack of exercise, it does not, in Merleau-Ponty's view, describe mass sociohistoric movements or the 'decisions' of people involved in them. 'What is known as the significance of events is not an idea which produces them . . . It is the concrete project of a future which is elaborated within social co-existence . . . before any personal decision is made' (Merleau-Ponty 2002, p. 449).

To illustrate his claim that not all situations are brought about by free, conscious choice, particularly those occurring at the communal level, Merleau-Ponty takes the example of social revolution: a phenomenon that he argues must be understood philosophically as a revolution in class-consciousness. According to Merleau-Ponty, only revolutionary intellectuals choose to become revolutionaries, but their intellectual project of revolution does not, by itself, bring about a revolution in class-consciousness. Unlike the revolutionary intellectual, the mass of ordinary people who become caught up in a revolutionary struggle do not choose to become revolutionaries. 'To make class-consciousness the outcome of a decision and a choice is to say that problems are solved on the day they are posed, that every question already contains the reply that it awaits' (Merleau-Ponty 2002, p. 446). To say that ordinary people choose to become revolutionaries is to suppose that they possess a particular kind of class-consciousness, a working-class class-consciousness for example, prior to a revolution, when in fact it is only through the collective 'existential project' (Merleau-Ponty 2002, p. 447) of social revolution that a particular kind of class-consciousness develops. The existential project of revolution, as opposed to the insufficient intellectual project, begins when a collective response to exploitation gathers momentum. At first this response is not articulated. 'It is prepared by some molecular process, it matures in coexistence before bursting forth into words and being related to objective ends' (Merleau-Ponty 2002, p. 446). It is not until the critical moment when ordinary people recognize the importance of representing and articulating their rapidly changing situation to themselves and to authority that they find a use for intellectuals. It is only later on, therefore, when the revolution has already begun to produce a particular kind of class-consciousness and made the social position of ordinary people an object of thought for them that they realize they have become revolutionaries. To summarize: prior to the revolution ordinary people are not in a position to represent the situation objectively or to make choices regarding it. During the revolution they react spontaneously. Only with the benefit of hindsight can they view their actions as though they were free, conscious choices that led to this or that end.

How can people choose a society that they have no clear idea of? The very idea of a new society emerges through revolution.

Merleau-Ponty's Marxist description of the development of class-consciousness is interesting, but is it valid as a criticism of Sartre's view that freedom is limitless? Arguably, Merleau-Ponty misrepresents Sartre when he suggests that he characterizes freedom not as an existential project, but as an intellectual project in which a person chooses those means, and only those means, that he perceives will bring about certain ends in a clearly represented future. As was emphasized earlier when Sartre's view of the future was examined, he categorically denies that the future is a representation (*BN*, p. 124). Merleau-Ponty fails to acknowledge this denial, overlooking the key passage in which it is made.[5] If the future is not a representation then choices cannot be determined by clearly envisaged ends. Admittedly, a person's so called 'chosen' ends may well guide and motivate his actions, but they do not determine them. Indeed, it can be argued that it is incorrect to separate choice and action in this way.

A person genuinely chooses an end only in so far as he acts to bring it about. For example, a man thought about going to London. He even made arrangements. In the end, however, he changed his mind and went to Manchester instead. It might be said that the man had chosen to go to London, as though his choice existed in some form prior to his acting. Strictly speaking, however, he had not chosen to go to London. He had thought about the possibility and made arrangements, undertaking certain actions that seemed to reveal certain parts of the supposed already existing concrete fact of his choice, but in reality choice must draw all its life from action. This is the existential truth behind the saying, 'Actions speak louder than words.' Only when the action is undertaken, well under way, or even completed, is it entirely correct to speak of the concrete fact of a choice to do *x*. Arguably, in saying that Sartre reduces freedom to an intellectual project Merleau-Ponty suggests that Sartre believes there are occasions when choice and action can be separated. Sartre, of course, does not believe this. It is central to his philosophy that choice is given reality and meaning only through action.

Represented as an intellectual project, Sartre's notion of freedom is found to be at fault, in that freedom is found to have limitations after all. That is, if free choice must always involve a choice of actions that aim to realize clearly envisaged ends, then not all actions can involve free choice, because not all actions that are undertaken can have clearly envisaged ends. Sartre, however, does not argue that free choice must involve a choice of actions that aim to realize clearly envisaged ends. Rather, his oft-repeated argument is that actions are undertaken primarily to overcome a perceived lack. The lack may be perceived without a person clearly envisaging the end that will be the overcoming of it. It is sufficient for the undertaking of action that the end aimed at be imagined in the most vague and nebulous of terms. Neither need there be any clear understanding of what actions will best realize an overcoming. The first tentative steps towards overcoming a perceived lack may be purely symbolic and of no practical benefit to the project of overcoming. It is a common view among existentialists that leaps in the dark, away from perceived lacks towards shadowy ends that it is hoped will overcome them, are no less free for being leaps in the dark. Indeed, for some existentialists there is no greater expression of freedom than leaping into the unknown. Sartre denies that a person is only free when he can rationalize what he is doing, intends to do, or has done, and limited in his freedom when he acts spontaneously. He is always free in that he is condemned to grasp every situation as lacking what is presently of value to him which he must choose to pursue or choose to deny himself.

A further criticism that Merleau-Ponty levels against Sartre in *Phenomenology of Perception* is to accuse him of positing a freedom that is free without having to be free. Or, at least, to accuse him of not acknowledging the full consequences of the fact that freedom has to be freedom. For Sartre, in terms of freedom, there is no difference between action and inaction, between choosing to act and choosing not to act: 'Not to choose is, in fact, to choose not to choose' (*BN*, p. 481). Though Merleau-Ponty understands and agrees with Sartre's claim, he nonetheless insists that a being that always chose to refuse to choose would not be free because it would not know itself as free. For Merleau-Ponty, in order to be free a being must 'Choose *something* in which [it sees], at least for a moment, a symbol of itself . . . The very notion of freedom demands that our decision should plunge into the future, that something should have been *done* by it' (Merleau-Ponty 2002, p. 437). A being that existed entirely as a self-overcoming and a complete self-denial would be blind to itself as a free overcoming of the objective world. According to Merleau-Ponty, choosing not to choose, choosing to do nothing, is possible only for a for-itself that knows what it is to choose to do something and to have done so. That is, freedom requires some experience of autonomy in order to know itself. A for-itself that never acted, never wanted to act and only ever exercised itself as a denial of itself, would have no experience of autonomy and hence no experience of itself.

Sartre would probably not dispute the logic of Merleau-Ponty's argument. Rather, he would challenge it on the grounds that it concerns a hypothetical case that could never be instantiated. He would argue that a for-itself that has no experience of itself is impossible, because a for-itself that has no experience of itself is simply not a for-itself. Consciousness must be transparent. It must be consciousness through and through. It must be conscious of being conscious. Imagine a person that could not act or had no desire to act: a person unrelentingly devoid of physical or verbal activity who lacked the self-awareness that Merleau-Ponty correctly insists emerges through action. Such a person would have to be in a persistent vegetative state and as such would not really be a person at all: not a for-itself.[6] A personality might be projected on to him by others, in much the same way as a child projects a personality on to a doll, particularly if he once had a personality, but this does not mean that he has a personality or is a person for himself. He is a non-person, a biological entity only: an in-itself.

As noted, some criticisms of Sartre's theory of freedom are weak and/or unfair, others are at least tenable, while some identify genuine problems. I will now consider some of the more serious criticisms of Sartre's theory of freedom.

In claiming that freedom is limitless Sartre is certainly not claiming that a person can always do exactly as he wishes: play football though he has no legs, fly though he has no wings. I have defended Sartre against criticisms based on this kind of simplistic interpretation of his views. However, not all criticisms of Sartre's limitless freedom thesis are so simplistic. Some criticisms set out a strong case for the view that responsibility and the ability to choose are less extensive than Sartre supposes. He is right that freedom cannot be limited by choosing not to choose; he is also right that helplessness in many situations is a sham; but is he right that people are always responsible for what they do and the evaluations they make? Merleau-Ponty, for one, thinks not. He seeks, for instance, to qualify Sartre's claim that a person is completely free to decide the meaning and value of objects in the world.

Recall once again Sartre's example of the mountain-crag. Sartre claims that a mountain-crag has its meaning and value conferred upon it by the person who encounters it (*BN*, p. 482). Merleau-Ponty is largely in agreement with Sartre on this point. As he says, 'When I say that this rock is unclimbable, it is certain that this attribute, like being big or little, straight or oblique, and indeed like all attributes in general, can be conferred upon it only by the project of climbing it, and by a human presence' (Merleau-Ponty 2002, p. 439).

Nonetheless, he goes on to argue that not all evaluation is simply a matter of abstract personal choice as Sartre suggests. In Merleau-Ponty's view there is a natural self based upon the natural limitations of the body and its basic physical relationship with the environment. The natural self limits freedom by rendering certain evaluations inevitable.

> Whether or not I have decided to climb them, these mountains appear high to me, because they exceed my body's power to take them in its stride . . . Underlying myself as a thinking subject . . . there is, therefore, as it were, a natural self which does not budge from its terrestrial situation and which constantly adumbrates absolute valuations . . . In so far as I have hands, feet, a body, I sustain around me intentions which are not dependent upon my decisions and which affect my surroundings in a way which I do not choose. (Merleau-Ponty 2002, pp. 439–40)

In considering Merleau-Ponty's notion of the natural self, John Compton argues that it provides a framework within which choices of value can be made: a framework of basic, non-intellectual, inescapable interpretations that inform, guide and influence deliberate choices of value.

> We are systems of body intentions before we are persons. Vital interests and skills pre-structure our interactions with the environment: they allow us to discover, as perceptually given, the initial resistances and cooperations of things; they dispose us to shared patterns of generally adaptive behaviour; and they constitute the general background against which deliberate choices are made and personal histories develop. This is what it means for us to be 'embodied' subjects: we are entangled in *real* situations, that is, relations of *reciprocal interpretations of meaning*, with the order of

nature, with other persons, and with institutions, through our bodies. (Compton 1982, p. 585)

In so far as Sartre's theory of freedom lacks any notion of a natural self, Merleau-Ponty is justified in arguing that he reduces freedom to an intellectual project. Sartre makes no reference to the existence of basic, non-intellectual, inescapable interpretations that pre-structure human interactions. This is arguably a serious weakness in his thesis because without them there appears to be nothing to prevent all evaluations that a person makes from being entirely arbitrary. If all the evaluations that a person makes are entirely arbitrary then there is nothing to maintain selfhood in so far as the self must be a reasonably consistent source of values in order to be.

In failing to acknowledge that interactions are pre-structured by the natural self, Sartre also overlooks various behavioural and dispositional phenomena that signify limitations to the capacity to choose. Examination of these various behavioural and dispositional phenomena reveals that not every conscious response, or every response that requires consciousness in order to be made, is freely chosen. It is precisely these various behavioural and dispositional phenomena that are considered both by V.J. McGill in 'Sartre's doctrine of freedom' and by Gregory McCulloch in *Using Sartre*. McGill considers sense of humour, panic reactions and mental disturbance, while McCulloch considers sexual preference.

McGill lists sense of humour among 'other things besides choice [that] are essential to human beings' (McGill 1949, p. 331). To find a joke amusing or not a person must be conscious, but it cannot be said that he chooses to find a joke amusing or not. Not least, if he had to decide whether or not he found a joke amusing he would not find it so because the spontaneity that is the hallmark of amusement would be lost. Admittedly, sense of humour is to a large extent a product of a person's background: a product of many past situations and the choices made in those situations. This point, however, does not damage the argument. Indeed, it shows how a present conscious response can be determined by a person's past, by his character. Against Sartre, it can be argued that there is a certain inertia in consciousness after all. This is not to say that a person has no control whatsoever over his sense of humour. Education, life experience and conscience may eventually lead him to find certain jokes which he used to find amusing, unamusing or even offensive. Nonetheless, if a person finds a joke amusing at a particular time he is not choosing to find it amusing, as though he could suddenly find it unamusing if he chose.

Regarding panic reactions McGill says, 'If modern infantry does not receive basic training, there is a large percentage of panic reactions, in spite of all good intentions' (McGill 1949, p. 333). Sartre would argue that if a soldier panics in face of an onslaught that is his choice. Such a claim shows an insensitivity to the propensities of what McGill describes as our 'psycho-biological nature or essence' (McGill 1949, p. 330). Panic has both a physical and a mental dimension. It is a physical response that requires consciousness in order to be made, but it is not always under the control of consciousness. Sometimes panic overwhelms consciousness. There is a fight-or-flight reaction over which a person, though he remains starkly conscious, has no control. The fact that a soldier can eventually learn to gain control over his panic reactions through training and experience, and hence place himself in a position to be able to choose not to panic, does not imply that every soldier, particularly the rookie, has the choice of whether or not to panic on a particular occasion.

Sartre has a lot to say about the phenomenon of fatigue. Can the same be said for fatigue as for panic reactions? Can Sartre's sissy, who quits a hike declaring himself overcome by fatigue (*BN*, pp. 454–5), be compared with the soldier who is overwhelmed by panic? Certainly, people are overwhelmed by fatigue. They collapse into unconsciousness or, despite genuine effort, they find further movement physically impossible. Yet this is not the same as saying that their consciousness has been overwhelmed by fatigue as by panic. They have simply ceased, at least temporarily, to be conscious or able-bodied. If they have not collapsed into unconsciousness then they are free to choose their response to their fatigue. To lie down and wait to die, to rest for a while, to try unsuccessfully to continue, and so on. Importantly, Sartre makes it clear that his sissy has not been overcome by fatigue in the form of unconsciousness or physical disability. Physically, he is as capable of continuing to hike as his equally fit companions. It seems reasonable to conclude then, as Sartre does, that a fatigue that does not involve genuine disability cannot force the sissy to quit. He chooses to quit and, therefore, could choose not to.

Still, how can the sissy choose to go on if he genuinely believes he has reached his physical limit? Arguably, it is irrelevant that a purely objective assessment of his fitness reveals that his belief is unjustified, as is the claim that his belief is the product of a free choice of himself. All that really matters, all that is required for him to be unable to continue, is that he believes he cannot continue. So long as he believes he cannot continue, and therefore does not do so, it is the case that he cannot continue. Those who doubt that belief can be so significant should remind themselves of the power that hypnosis has both to enable and disable.[7] The sissy's belief that he cannot continue is a form of self-hypnosis. Ironically, one way to break this self-hypnosis and reveal to him that he could choose to continue is to force him to do so.

Responding to the above argument, Sartre would probably insist that although the genuine belief produced by hypnosis can incapacitate people, his sissy does not genuinely believe he has reached his physical limit. His belief that he cannot go on is not a form of hypnosis. Rather, it is a belief held in bad faith that serves his own self-interest. He does not want to know what he is capable of because he does not want to go on. However, because not wanting to go on characterizes him as lazy, he prefers to believe that he cannot go on.

Regarding mental illness McGill says, 'If every human being freely chooses to be what he is, then neurotics and psychotics of all kinds and descriptions, are equally responsible for their condition' (McGill 1949, p. 338). McGill argues that this goes against the accumulated evidence of psychiatrists who have long distinguished fakers from the genuinely disturbed on the grounds that the latter, unlike the former, have certain obsessive, compulsive tendencies over which they have little or no control. It appears to be a weakness of Sartre's theory of freedom that it cannot allow for that element of diminished responsibility that is the generally accepted hallmark of insanity.

Considering sexual preference McCulloch acknowledges that 'sexuality is the sort of thing that has to be taken responsibility for' (McCulloch 1994, p. 67). By this he means that sane people are responsible for the actions that stem from their sexual preferences. He argues, however, that people are not responsible for their sexual preferences. They do not choose them and cannot choose to change them. Homosexuals, for example, do not choose to find themselves sexually attracted to members of their own sex, any more than heterosexuals choose to find themselves attracted to members of the opposite sex. 'Not everything that makes a person what they are, and is a source of responsibility, is something they chose' (McCulloch 1994, p. 66). It seems a person's particular physiological nature limits their freedom by rendering certain preferences, sexual or otherwise, unavoidable. This claim echoes Merleau-Ponty's claim that the natural self limits freedom by rendering certain evaluations inevitable.

I want, finally, to explore what is perhaps the most serious flaw in Sartre's theory of freedom. It is widely held by Sartre's critics that choice, as Sartre conceives it, is groundless. Certainly, he argues that beliefs and convictions about the best course of action to take in a particular situation cannot provide grounds for choosing because they reflect values that are themselves the product of a groundless choice. As he says, 'my freedom is the unique foundation of values, and *nothing*, absolutely nothing, justifies my adoption of this or that value, this or that scale of values' (*BN*, p. 38) and 'we have neither behind us, nor before us in a luminous realm of values, any means of justification or excuse' (*EAH*, p. 34).

For Sartre, choice is always radical. He illustrates radical choice with the example of a student of his who faces the dilemma of leaving home to fight for the resistance or staying home to take care of his afflicted mother (*EAH*, pp. 35–8). There is no question that the student must reach a decision, yet there are, according to Sartre, no grounds for deciding which course of action to take: '. . . I can neither seek within myself for an authentic impulse to action, nor can I expect, from some ethic, formulae that will enable me to act' (*EAH*, p. 37). The student is in a 'state of abandonment' (*EAH*, p. 35), 'condemned to be free' (*BN*, pp. 129, 439; *EAH*, p. 34), and must, therefore, make an arbitrary decision. He must plunge into one or other course of action without reason or justification.

Sartre's general claim is that ultimately choice is always and unavoidably based upon wholly arbitrary decisions. 'You are free, therefore choose – that is to say, invent' (*EAH*, p. 38). Furthermore, he is of the opinion that if a choice could be guided and influenced in any way by beliefs, convictions or values it would be a caused phenomenon rather than a genuinely free choice. Sartre, mistakenly according to many critics, does not allow that choices can in some sense be caused and yet remain choices. In defending his claim that people must always choose in face of their facticity, that if their facticity determined their choices people would be stripped of their freedom and reduced to cogs in a machine, Sartre, to the detriment of his thesis, goes too far in insisting that ultimately there can be no influences upon choice whatsoever.

Sartre favours the notion that all choices are ultimately groundless partly because, in his view, it reveals the profound extent of human freedom.[8] Arguing against this radically libertarian stance, McGill insists that it serves to 'depreciate the role of past and present stimuli to the point where choice becomes a mystery' (McGill 1949, p. 334). Other critics, C.W. Robbins for example, argue that it completely undermines the possibility of moral agency: 'The consequence of Sartre's reduction of the role of deliberation is to exclude all forms of the moral life' (Robbins 1977, p. 119).

Choice, as Sartre conceives it, is a mysterious phenomenon because he offers no explanation of why a person faced with options that have only the value he chooses to grant them, chooses one course of action rather than another. Even if it is the case that the person bases all his choices on the toss of a coin, still nothing is explained. An explanation is still required as to why he chooses to attribute value to and abide by the 'decision' of a coin. It would be a wholly inadequate explanation of his decision to abide by the 'decision' of a coin simply to say that he decided to do so.

As to the claim that Sartre's conception of choice undermines the possibility of moral agency, simply note that if tossing a coin is as good a way as any other of solving a moral dilemma, then it is not possible for a person to act in a way that can be described as moral. To plunge randomly into a particular course of action cannot be considered moral because a morality that permits any action whatsoever is not a morality. If a person made it a moral principle to solve moral dilemmas with the toss of a coin he would not be a moral person, but rather a person who had forgone moral considerations in order to reach decisions. If moral values are groundless and have no more significance in the decision-making process than tossing a coin, throwing a dice or cutting a pack of cards, then the distinction between moral, amoral and immoral is lost.

Wittgenstein argues against the possibility of a private language in his *Philosophical Investigations* (passages 269–75). Applying Wittgenstein's theory to morality, Anthony Manser argues that distinctions between moral, amoral and immoral must be made in accordance with rules that are, or could be, publicly intelligible (Manser 1981, p. 142). A private morality in which moral distinctions are made in accordance with a person's whims is unintelligible as a morality because the 'rules' of this morality, being arbitrary and inconsistent, are unrecognizable as rules.

Of course, that Sartre's view of choice excludes the possibility of moral agency is not necessarily a criticism of his position. It can be argued that moral values are illusory and that, therefore, genuine moral agency *is* impossible. Despite several attempts to produce an existentialist ethics, Sartre sceptically concludes that 'Ethics is both necessary and impossible' (*SG*, p. 247). Unfortunately, it is beyond the scope of this book to examine the large and controversial claim that ethics is impossible. It must suffice to say that in so far as Sartre's view of choice excludes the possibility of genuine moral agency, it is at least consistent with the general, underlying amorality of his existentialism.

The charge, of course, is not simply that Sartre's theory of freedom excludes moral grounds for choice, but that it excludes grounds for choice altogether. This charge is particularly damaging because it seems to imply that in fact Sartre's theory of freedom sheds no light at all upon the phenomenon of choosing. Recall McGill's claim that Sartre depreciates choice to the level of a mysterious phenomenon. It is doubtful that Sartre can be defended against this charge, particularly when he even rules out such basic grounds for choice as instinct and feeling. 'Feeling is formed by the deeds that one does; therefore I cannot consult it as a guide to action' (*EAH*, p. 37). Almost certainly, Sartre's view of choice, which threatens to undermine the whole edifice of his theory of freedom, is badly in need of some notion of a pre-structure. That is, some notion of a framework, perhaps based on Merleau-Ponty's concept of the natural self, within which choices can be made that are more than arbitrary.

PART 3

BAD FAITH

CHAPTER 5

THE PHENOMENON OF BAD FAITH

> If bad faith is possible, it is because it is an immediate, permanent threat to every project of the human being; it is because consciousness conceals in its being a permanent risk of bad faith. The origin of this risk is the fact that the nature of consciousness simultaneously is to be what it is not and not to be what it is.
>
> (*BN*, p. 70)

Freedom gives rise directly to the possibility of bad faith. This is so because bad faith involves an attempt on the part of the for-itself – a being that must perpetually choose itself – to choose itself as a being that need not or cannot choose itself. Clearly, a being that chooses itself as a being that need not or cannot choose itself must ultimately fail in this chosen aim by virtue of the very fact that this aim is chosen: 'Not to choose is, in fact, to choose not to choose' (*BN*, p. 481).

Recall that the for-itself cannot simply choose itself as *x* and thus become *x* once and for all, but must rather perpetually choose and reaffirm itself as *x* against the ever-present possibility of ceasing to choose itself as *x*. As noted, the for-itself is what it is not and can never be what it is; it can never coincide with itself. If the for-itself were what it is then bad faith would be impossible as an attempt on the part of the for-itself to be what it is. A person cannot try to be what he is, only what he is not. 'If man is what he is, bad faith is forever impossible and candour ceases to be his ideal and becomes instead his being' (*BN*, p. 58).

The above paragraph provides only a preliminary outline of what bad faith is. A comprehensive account of the phenomenon requires a detailed examination of its various ontological structures. These structures are intelligible only in light of the account of Sartre's phenomenology of consciousness and freedom already provided. As indicated at the start of this book, bad faith must follow consciousness and freedom in order of explanation if it is not to be thoroughly misunderstood. Failure to identify and evaluate bad faith firmly within the broader context of Sartre's phenomenology has led some commentators to misrepresent and oversimplify the phenomenon.

The most prevalent and most damaging misrepresentation of bad faith arising from the failure fully to appreciate its phenomenological context is that bad faith is equivalent to self-deception. Distinguishing bad faith from self-deception is a good way to begin examining the various ontological structures of bad faith. Apart from removing the most serious obstacle to a clear understanding of bad faith, distinguishing bad faith from self-deception facilitates the accurate interpretation of Sartre's concrete examples of bad faith. Sartre's concrete examples of bad faith – the flirt, the waiter, and so on – play a central role in his account of bad faith. A proper understanding of these concrete examples is the key to a proper understanding of the several interrelated forms of bad faith as they are played out in the diverse dramas of everyday human life.

BAD FAITH AND SELF-DECEPTION

To define bad faith as self-deception is a confusing oversimplification, even if this definition has certain uses as a first approximation. As will be seen, bad faith often looks like self-deception even though it is not. To show that bad faith is not self-deception it is necessary to examine self-deception. The most logical and productive way to examine self-deception is to compare it with deception: that broader phenomenon of which self-deception is supposedly a subspecies.

Both deception and self-deception involve denying that something is the case; they both involve a 'negative attitude' (*BN*, p. 48). The negative attitude of deception, however, unlike self-deception, has no bearing on consciousness itself. 'The essence of the lie implies in fact that the liar actually is in complete possession of the truth which he is hiding . . . The liar intends to deceive and he does not seek to hide this intention from himself nor to disguise the translucency of consciousness' (*BN*, p. 48). Deception – the straightforward lie – aims at deceiving the Other, and relies upon 'the Ontological duality of myself and myself in the eyes of the Other' (*BN*, p. 49). Deception succeeds because for the Other my consciousness is a consciousness that the Other is not conscious of. There is a genuine external relation involved. Within the unity of a single consciousness, however, there are no external relations or dualities.[1] 'The duality of the deceiver and the deceived does not exist here' (*BN*, p. 49).

My earlier examination of self-reflection revealed that it is incorrect to view a single consciousness as though it were two externally related for-itselves. There cannot be a duality of deceiver and deceived within a single consciousness any more than there can be a duality of reflective and reflected-on.[2] If a person intentionally undertakes to deceive himself he unavoidably catches himself in the act. 'We must agree in fact that if I deliberately and cynically attempt to lie to myself, I fail completely in this undertaking; the lie falls back and collapses beneath my look' (*BN*, p. 49). It cannot be correct, therefore, to equate bad faith with self-deception conceived in terms of a deceiver–deceived duality. A person cannot both know and not know something at the same time. The notion of a straightforward deceiver–deceived duality within a single consciousness is contradictory.

The contradiction inherent in the notion of lying to oneself that Sartre identifies is also identified by Raphael Demos in 'Lying to oneself' and by Herbert Fingarette in *Self-Deception*. Demos attempts to avoid the contradiction by arguing that self-deception involves a person holding two contradictory beliefs one of which he does not notice. He denies that this implies a duality within consciousness. More specifically, he denies that it implies the Freudian duality of conscious and unconscious. Demos insists that 'The belief and the disbelief are simultaneous and both exist in the consciousness of the person' (Demos 1960, p. 592).

Fingarette acknowledges that Demos correctly identifies the contradiction inherent in the notion of self-deception. He argues, however, that Demos's notion of not noticing does nothing to overcome this contradiction. In Fingarette's view, the central problem with Demos's thesis is that a genuine case of not noticing is not a case of self-deception, because the intent that characterizes the notion of self-deception is lacking. Fingarette notes that there is no deep paradox involved in holding beliefs that are incompatible and not noticing that they are incompatible. Not noticing that my beliefs are incompatible signifies ignorance rather than self-deception.

We all no doubt have such beliefs, if only because we cannot see far enough into the implications of each of our beliefs. The child, the intellectually naïve and the intellectually careless no doubt commonly hold beliefs which involve direct contradiction. If this were all that were involved in self-deception, who would be puzzled by it? (Fingarette 2000, p. 15)

In a genuine case of self-deception a person must in some sense have already appreciated the incompatibility of his beliefs. Rather than simply not notice this incompatibility he must somehow deliberately ignore it. Fingarette argues that Demos fails to distinguish between not noticing and deliberately ignoring even though he employs both phrases. Demos is aware that there is a contradiction involved in the claim that a person can deliberately ignore what he is conscious of, but his efforts to tackle this contradiction are misdirected towards the phenomenon of not noticing incompatible beliefs: a phenomenon that, according to Fingarette, should not be confused with self-deception.

Fingarette formulates an alternative account of self-deception that seeks to overcome the contradiction that Demos fails to tackle. Fingarette acknowledges that this account is akin to Sartre's account of bad faith. The similarity between the positions of Fingarette and Sartre will be explored in due course as part of an examination of the faith of bad faith. As will be seen, Fingarette's notion of not spelling-out and Sartre's notion of the primitive project of bad faith are virtually identical.

Sartre's general claim is that bad faith should not be equated with self-deception, particularly if 'self-deception' is meant to refer to the operations of a deceiver–deceived duality within a single consciousness. In rejecting this duality Sartre more specifically rejects as illogical Freud's duality of conscious and unconscious. Sartre's disagreement with Freud is worth considering both for its own sake and as a further step towards understanding the phenomenon of bad faith.

Freud argues in *The Ego and the Id*, and elsewhere, that self-deception is possible because the ego (the conscious mind) is capable of repressing certain distasteful truths, beliefs and desires. That is, it is capable of preventing certain thoughts emerging into the light of consciousness from the id (the unconscious mind, the seat of primitive drives and instincts). In short, Freud argues that the ego is capable of exercising censorship.

We have formed the idea that in each individual there is a coherent organisation of mental processes; and we call this his *ego*. It is to this ego that consciousness is attached; . . . it is the mental agency which supervises all its own constituent processes, and which goes to sleep at night, though even then it exercises the censorship on dreams. From this ego proceed the repressions, too, by means of which it is sought to exclude certain trends in the mind not merely from consciousness but from other forms of effectiveness and activity. In analysis these trends which have been shut out stand in opposition to the ego, and the analysis is faced with the task of removing the resistances which the ego displays against concerning itself with the repressed. (Freud 1986, p. 443)

Sartre objects to Freud's position as expressed in the above passage on the grounds that consciousness is never opaque but always transparent. He argues that to be conscious of a thought is to be conscious of it through and through because a thought exists only in so far as a person is conscious of it. Sartre, therefore, does not accept what Freud's notion of censorship implies: that a person can be both conscious and yet not conscious of a particular thought.

If we reject the language and the materialistic mythology of psychoanalysis, we perceive that the censor [the ego] in order to apply its activity with discernment must know what it is repressing . . . In a word, how could the censor discern the impulses needing to be repressed without being conscious of discerning them? (*BN*, pp. 52–3)

Freud contradicts himself in claiming that a person can deliberately push an idea or a desire into the unconscious, yet be unaware that he is doing so. This contradictory claim, incidentally, is not to be confused with the non-contradictory claim that a person can both know something and yet not be presently conscious of it.[3] Freud's account of self-deception, in supposing a psychic duality that allows for the operation of self-censorship, is untenable and unable to shed light on the phenomenon of self-deception.

Arguably, Sartre's account of bad faith offers the only account of so-called self-deception that does not appeal to the problematic notion of a duality within consciousness. It rejects any notion of psychic duality in favour of the notion of the 'double property of the human being' (*BN*, p. 56) as both subject and object. To make sense of Sartre's account it must be recalled that the for-itself lacks coincidence with itself and is a free, transcendent flight towards the future. It must also be recalled that the body constitutes the immediate facticity of the human being that the for-itself perpetually transcends without being able finally to transcend it. A person, as noted, is both subject and object: a subject in so far as his consciousness transcends the world (his being-in-the-world) and a transcended object in so far as his body is in the world amongst other objects (his being-in-the-midst-of-the-world). Bad faith, or what might crudely be termed 'self-deception', is, or is achieved through, subtle and ongoing manipulations of this subject–object double property. More specifically, bad faith is, or is achieved through, attempted selective inversions of facticity and transcendence. Bad faith is not a state. Rather, like the for-itself that realizes it, it is an an ongoing project that must sustain itself against the constant threat of collapse. Sartre describes bad faith as having a metastable structure (*BN*, p. 68).[4]

As all the 'various aspects' (*BN*, p. 56) or types of bad faith are realized through inversions and manipulations of facticity and transcendence, an understanding of these inversions and manipulations is essential to an understanding of bad faith. Sartre explores the various aspects or types of bad faith through a series of concrete examples that I will now examine in turn, beginning with the example of the flirt or coquette (*BN*, p. 55).[4]

RELINQUISHING RESPONSIBILITY – THE FLIRT

Sartre describes a situation in which a man compliments a woman and pays her polite attentions that she takes at face value refusing to acknowledge their 'sexual background' (*BN*, p. 55). Eventually, the man takes the woman's hand.

> This act of her companion risks changing the situation by calling for an immediate decision. To leave the hand there is to consent in herself to flirt, to engage herself. To withdraw is to break the troubled and unstable harmony which gives the hour its charm. The aim is to postpone the moment of decision as long as possible. We know what happens next; the young woman leaves her hand there, but she does not notice that she is leaving it. She does

not notice because it happens by chance that she is at this moment all intellect. She draws her companion up to the most lofty regions of sentimental speculation; she speaks of life, of her life, she shows herself in her essential aspect – a personality, a consciousness. And during this time the divorce of the body from the soul is accomplished; the hand rests inert between the warm hands of her companion – neither consenting nor resisting – a thing. (*BN*, p. 55)

The woman leaves her hand in the hand of the man without facing up to what is implied by holding hands: the new situation it reveals. How does she achieve this postponement of decision? She achieves it by treating her hand as a mere object rather than as that which directly expresses her subjectivity through its activity, and by treating her act of omission of leaving her hand in the hand of the man as though it were not an action. Treated as an object her hand is exempted from acting, from revealing the situation through its action and from revealing the woman to herself. Objects do not act, they are acted upon, but hands are not objects in so far as they directly express the consciousness to which they belong. When a person is conscious and in control of her limbs (i.e., she does not suffer from involuntary jerks, and so on), whatever her hands do or do not do are her actions for which she alone is responsible. A person's hands, a person's body, are part and parcel of an embodied consciousness that has its being through the active transcendence of its embodiment.

If bad faith is to be characterized other than in terms of a deceiver–deceived duality it must be recognized that the woman knows her hand is held and what this implies. Yet somehow she evades this knowledge. In so far as she knows it, it cannot be said that she has succeeded in evading it, rather she is the ongoing project of seeking to evade it and distract herself from it. Bad faith is self-distraction rather than self-deception. The term 'deception' suggests a liar, but consider the way in which a magician deceives us. The hand is quicker than the eye because the magician employs techniques to distract us.

The woman distracts herself from the meaning of her situation, from the meaning of the disposition of her limbs and from her responsibility for their meaningful disposition by fleeing herself towards the future. Each moment she aims to become a being beyond her situated self, the meaning of which would not be her current situation. That is, she aims to become a being beyond the situated for-itself: a for-itself-in-itself. Such a being would not be subject to the demands of the situation. It would not be obliged to act, to choose. She abandons her hands, her whole body, to the past. She hopes to leave it all behind her as so much dead weight. Yet, in the very act of abandoning it, she re-apprehends the situation of her body – *her* situation, *her* facticity – as a demand to choose. To take the man's hand willingly or to withdraw, that is the choice. But she meets this demand for positive choice and action with a choice of herself as a being that would be beyond the requirement to choose. She chooses herself as a flight from choice towards a would-be being beyond choice. It is this negative choice that exercises her, that distracts her, that stands in for the positive choice she knows her situation demands. She avoids making this positive choice by choosing herself as a person who is about to completely transcend her responsibility for her embodied, situated self; she chooses herself as a being who is about to completely escape its facticity.

It is now possible to give a full account of that all-important inversion of facticity and transcendence that I claimed above lies at the heart of bad faith. While she is involved in this precarious project of bad faith the woman treats the facticity of her situation, in terms of which her choices of herself should be exercised, as a transcendent power over her: as though it belonged to the Other for whom she is an object. That is, she treats her facticity as though it is a transcendence. At the same time, she treats her transcendent consciousness as though it is its own transcendence: as though it is a transcendence-in-itself rather than the transcendence of the facticity of her situation. She treats it as though it is a transcendence finally transcended by itself. That is, she treats her transcendence as though it is a facticity. This perpetual appearance of being a transcendence finally transcended by itself, a transcendence in-itself, is, however, perpetually annihilated on the grounds that a transcendence must necessarily be a transcendence of something other than itself. It can only be a transcendence of itself as something other than itself (i.e., a transcendence of itself as past). For it to cease to transcend would be for it to cease to be that which has its being through perpetual becoming. '[Bad faith] is a certain art of forming contradictory concepts which unite in themselves both an idea and the negation of that idea' (*BN*, p. 56).

Bad faith involves misrepresenting facticity as transcendence and transcendence as facticity. Sartre makes this point clear in a passage that perhaps more than any other in *Being and Nothingness* reveals the ontological crux of bad faith:

> The basic concept which is thus engendered, utilises the double property of the human being, who is at once a facticity and a transcendence. These two aspects of human reality are and ought to be capable of a valid coordination. But bad faith does not wish either to coordinate them nor to surmount them in a synthesis. Bad faith seeks to affirm their identity while preserving their differences. It must affirm facticity as being transcendence and transcendence as being facticity, in such a way that at the instant when a person apprehends the one, he can find himself abruptly faced with the other. (*BN*, p. 56)

To summarize. The for-itself strives to ignore the facticity of its situation by preoccupying itself with striving to render its own transcendence transcended. The for-itself concerns itself with itself, and all else – the situation, the body – is abandoned as alien and meaningless. A person in bad faith avoids responsibility for his embodied situation by denying that it is his situation. He treats his situation and himself as meaningless from his own point of view and considers that all is meaningful only from the point of view of the Other.[5]

The example of the flirt presents one way of being in bad faith, but by no means the only way. It is important to note that there are several related forms of bad faith that Sartre considers through his various examples: the flirt (*BN*, pp. 55–6), the waiter (*BN*, pp. 59–60), the sad person (*BN*, pp. 60–1), the homosexual and his friend (*BN*, pp. 63–5) and the coward (*BN*, pp. 66–7). As already indicated, no account of bad faith would be complete that did not consider the several related forms of bad faith exemplified by these various characters. The several related forms of bad faith are distinguishable in terms of the various ways in which the person concerned plays with the aforementioned 'double property of the human being, who is at once a facticity and a transcendence' (*BN*, p. 56). For instance, whereas the flirt seeks a complete separation of her facticity and her transcendence, Sartre's waiter, it has been traditionally argued, seeks to become his facticity so as to preclude his transcendence.

AUTOMATON OR ACTOR? – THE WAITER

Sartre conjures up a vivid picture of the waiter in action, offering a rich description of the man's exaggerated movements and gestures. 'His movement is quick and forward, a little too precise, a little too rapid. He comes toward the patrons with a step a little too quick. He bends forward a little too eagerly, his voice, his eyes express an interest a little too solicitous for the order of the customer' (*BN*, p. 59). The waiter comports himself in a deliberate and calculated manner, walking with a robotic stiffness and restraining his movements as though he were a machine; a thing rather than a person. Sartre concludes that his waiter is playing at being a waiter:[6] 'the waiter in the café plays with his condition in order to realize it' (*BN*, p. 59).

His aim is to be a waiter in the same way that a table is a table. His aim is to deny his transcendence and the fact that he has to be what he is without being able to be it by attempting to realize himself as the being-in-itself of a waiter. He overacts his role as a waiter in order to convince himself that he is a waiter-thing.[7]

In so far as the waiter aims to be convinced by his own performance, it is important to him that his performance convinces others. The more others are convinced that he is nothing more than a waiter, the more he himself will be convinced, because it is from their point of view, and their point of view alone, that he strives to see himself. He strives to see himself from the point of view of others for whom he *is* a waiter. He is a waiter for others in the mode of being what he is so long as nothing about his behaviour suggests that he might be something else. Hence, he is meticulous in his performance. He has no wish to let his guard down because to cast doubt about his identity in the minds of his patrons – his audience – would be to cast doubt in his own mind. His task is made easier by the fact that others, in their desire for a regular and predictable world free from sources of anguish, are disposed towards seeing him as a waiter and nothing more than a waiter. There is a sense in which he is obliged by his clientele to convince them that he is nothing but a waiter, otherwise he might offend their cosy expectations: 'A grocer who dreams is offensive to the buyer, because such a grocer is not wholly a grocer' (*BN*, p. 59).

Recall that from the point of view of others, a person is a transcendence-transcended. The waiter's aim, it can be argued, is to become this transcendence-transcended *for himself*: to become his own facticity. He strives to be at one with his own representation of himself, but the very fact that he has to represent to himself what he is means that he cannot be it.

> It is a 'representation' for others and for myself [if I am the waiter in question], which means that I can be he only in representation. But if I represent myself as him, I am not he; I am separated from him as the object from the subject, separated by *nothing*, but this nothing isolates me from him. I can not be he, I can only play at being him; that is, imagine to myself that I am he. And thereby I affect him with nothingness. (*BN*, p. 60)

The example of the waiter who strives in vain to be a waiter as a table is a table – a waiter-thing – once again confirms Sartre's central maxim that the being of the for-itself is to be what it is not and not to be what it is. In concluding his example of the waiter Sartre says, 'if I am one [a waiter], this can not be in the mode of being-in-itself. I am a waiter in the mode of *being what I am not*' (*BN*, p. 60).

The traditional view of Sartre's waiter is that he strives to be the being-in-itself of a waiter so as to escape his freedom and indeterminacy and the anguish they cause him – a project that places him in bad faith. Certainly, striving to be a thing so as to escape the burden of freedom is an identifiable form of bad faith. However, against the traditional view of Sartre's waiter it can be argued that although the waiter does indeed strive to be a waiter-thing, he is not in bad faith because the purpose of his striving is not to escape his freedom. Arguably, his motives are entirely different from those of a person in bad faith.[8] Arguably, he is no more in bad faith for trying to be a waiter than an actor is in bad faith for trying to be Hamlet.

A person who tries to be a waiter or Hamlet by playing at being a waiter or Hamlet to the best of his ability is not trying to become and does not consider himself to be a waiter or Hamlet. We draw a sharp distinction between the great actor who convinces us that he is Hamlet and the madman who thinks that he is Hamlet. Of course, when we say that the great actor convinces us that he is Hamlet, we do not mean to say that we literally believe he is Hamlet. We know Hamlet is a fictional character, and even if Hamlet were not a fictional character, we know that the actor is only an actor. A great actor enables us to suspend our disbelief that he is Hamlet. He so absorbs us in a performance in which he himself is absorbed that for a time we simply do not reflect upon the fact that he is not Hamlet. We do not believe that he is Hamlet, but neither do we disbelieve that he is Hamlet – at least, not until after the performance when reflection forces us to acknowledge that we have been involved in a make-believe situation. As Shakespeare is fond of pointing out, every situation, in a certain sense, involves an element of make-believe – the stage, the café, the lecture theatre, and so on.

All the world's a stage,
And all the men and women merely players;
They have their exits and their entrances,
And one man in his time plays many parts
(*As You Like It*, II, vii)

Consider a public speaker, a lecturer for example. Though a lecturer does not play a part as the actor plays a part, a good lecturer nonetheless performs his role. 'The good speaker is the one who plays at speaking, because he can not be speaking [*be* a speaker]' (*BN*, p. 60).

The good lecturer makes-believe he is a creature born to lecture rather than a person who is a lecturer in the mode of being what he is not. True, he is a lecturer in the mode of being what he is not, but this does not mean that what he really is, beneath the pretence of being a lecturer, is a nothingness-in-itself. The performance of a lecturer who takes himself to be nothing, least of all a lecturer, is dull and unconvincing because his project of being his own nothingness detracts from his project of performing his role as a lecturer. Furthermore, far from being in good faith, such a nihilistic person who constantly tells himself that he is in fact nothing is actually in bad faith. His bad faith consists in his (false) belief that he is his own nothingness in the mode of being it, a nothingness-in-itself, when in fact his nothingness is a being-for-itself which he has to be without being able to be it. For a person to believe that 'deep down' he is a non-being-in-itself is equivalent to believing that 'deep down' he is a being-in-itself. In so far as both attitudes involve considering himself to be a self-identical being, both attitudes are equally in bad faith. In *The Ethics of Ambiguity*, Simone de Beauvoir compares the nihilist with the serious person who seeks to annihilate his subjectivity by treating himself as an object defined by social norms:

> This failure of the serious sometimes brings about a radical disorder. Conscious of being unable to be anything, man then decides to be nothing. We shall call this attitude nihilistic. The nihilist is close to the spirit of seriousness, for instead of realising his negativity as a living movement, he conceives his annihilation in a substantial way. He wants to *be* nothing, and this nothing that he dreams of is still another sort of being. (de Beauvoir 2000, p. 52)

I have considered the good lecturer who throws himself wholeheartedly into his performance, and the dull lecturer whose performance suffers because his belief that he is a non-being-in-itself discourages him from playing at being a lecturer. I will now consider a lecturer whose performance suffers, not because he believes he is a non-being-in-itself but because he believes (while he is lecturing) that he is really something other than a person who plays at being a lecturer. Almost anyone who has ever lectured can identify with that embarrassing moment when self-reflection upon the sound of their own voice and their pretence of being a lecturer-thing shatters the make-believe and prevents them from continuing. Arguably, it is during such a moment of self-consciousness that a person is in bad faith, rather than when they are pretending to be a lecturer-thing. In bad faith they assume that their supposed true self has caught itself in the act of pretending to be what it is not. In bad faith this supposed true self is then perturbed and embarrassed by its insincerity. Bad faith is involved here because there is no such entity as a true self that is what it is without having to be what it is. A person who fails to recognize that he is never what he is, but has, rather, to be what he is; a person who believes that to play with his condition in order to realize it is insincerity; is a sincere person. But as Sartre points out, sincerity is a phenomenon of bad faith that has the same basic structure as bad faith. This important point will be explored further in due course.

A closer reading of Sartre's description of the waiter reveals that, just like the good actor or lecturer, there is a definite sense in which the waiter is aware of what he is doing. His 'tongue is in his cheek'. (*Tongue in cheek* = with insincere or ironical intent.) He is consciously – though not self-consciously – doing an impression of a waiter; a good impression that, like all good impressions, is more like

x than x himself. Indeed, it is an impression that he has so refined that it is second nature to him. To claim that acting like a waiter is second nature to him is not to claim that he believes he has become a waiter. Rather, it is to claim that he has become his performance; become it in the sense that when he is absorbed in his performance he does not reflect upon the fact that he is performing. Sartre writes, 'the waiter in the café plays with his condition in order to realise it' (*BN*, p. 59). By this he does not mean that the waiter plays with his condition in order to become it, but rather that his condition is only ever realized as a playing with his condition. The waiter knows full well that he can never be identical with his condition because in order to 'be' his condition he must play at being it.

With regard to playing at being what we are not – a waiter, Hamlet, a lecturer, a madman, and so on – there are useful insights to be gained from considering the character of Hamlet as it develops through the play. Hamlet is made increasingly aware as the play progresses that there is no such thing as the true Hamlet, that it is impossible to distinguish between being himself and playing a role. Hamlet's futile search for his true self mocks the advice that Polonius gives to his son, Laertes: 'This above all: to thine own self be true' (*Hamlet*, I, iii).

Is Hamlet mad or is he playing a role? 'Though this be madness, yet there is method in't' (*Hamlet*, II, ii). This remark from Polonius regarding Hamlet's behaviour emphasizes the possibility that Hamlet is mad despite having undertaken to behave as if mad on purpose. But what, as the characters in the play ask, is it to be mad? Is it to *be* mad as a table is a table? Is it to behave madly? Is it to consider oneself mad? Is it, perhaps, to consider oneself sane, as Hamlet does initially? Confronted by the difficulty of providing a satisfactory answer to this question, Polonius answers with a truism that he evidently knows is unsatisfactory, and by so doing implies that whatever madness is, it is never simply madness in itself.

> I will be brief. Your noble son is mad –
> 'Mad' call I it; for to define true madness,
> What is't but to be nothing else but mad?
> But let that go.
>
> (*Hamlet*, II, ii)

In a sense, of course, there is no doubt that a person *is* mad who takes his old friend the Lord Chamberlain to be a fishmonger

(*Hamlet*, II, ii), just as a person who is Hamlet *is* the mad Prince of Denmark, just as a person who serves in a café *is* a waiter. What else do we call a man who serves food and drink in a café for a wage? 'there is no doubt that I am in a sense a café waiter [if I am the waiter in question] – otherwise could I not just as well call myself a diplomat or a reporter?' (*BN*, p. 60). In so far as people are identified with and identify themselves with their occupation (or lack of occupation), the waiter is certainly a waiter. In answer to the question, 'What are you?', anyone whose occupation is to serve customers in a café is likely to answer, 'I am a waiter.' Whether or not they identify themselves with their occupation, they will almost certainly give this answer because the question 'What are you?' is most often asked with the intention of discovering a person's occupation. Very rarely is 'What are you?' asked in the deep philosophical sense of 'What are you *really*?' Perhaps the reason for this is that 'What are you *really*?' is an impossible question to answer. Furthermore, any attempt to answer this question affirmatively is likely to lead a person into bad faith in the form of sincerity.

Although 'What are you?' is most often another way of saying 'What do you do?', it is generally believed that what a person does by way of occupation reveals much about the kind of person they are: their tastes, habits, intelligence, sex appeal, and so on. Evidently, members of prestigious professions are far happier identifying themselves with what they do than are members of low-status professions. Seldom do lawyers, doctors, film-producers or astronauts disclaim 'It's just a job. A job's a job.' People in less-respected employment, on the other hand, are often keen to seize upon the truth that a person is not what he does in the mode of being it. 'I am not really a toilet-cleaner', insists the young hopeful. 'That is just my job. I am really a budding author.'

The young hopeful who identifies himself as a budding author rather than as a toilet-cleaner chooses to recognize his transcendence in so far as it allows him to distance himself from a job he is ashamed of, but he ignores his transcendence and falls into bad faith in so far as he chooses to identify himself with a pastime he is proud of. As it is impossible to be what we are in the mode of being it, the young hopeful is not a budding author in the mode of being one just as he is not a toilet-cleaner in the mode of being one.

Anyone of ambition forced by circumstances to do a menial job is likely to fall into bad faith in the way referred to. If nothing else, such an attitude helps to stave off anguish more effectively than simply accepting that today I clean toilets while tomorrow there is a chance that I may publish a successful novel. Few things make an ambitious person who has not yet made the big time more anxious than the thought that if he dies today then posterity will remember him simply as a menial.

Heidegger notes that the thought of death does not simply inspire fear – fear of the unknown, fear of physical annihilation – but also anguish: 'Being-towards-death is essentially anxiety' (Heidegger 1993, p. 310). Death, as the ultimate limit of all possibility, represents the final limitation to a person's ability to transcend, overcome and perfect himself according to his ideal. Not that immortality would allow a person to perfect himself and become one with himself. As Sartre notes (*BN*, p. 546), even if a person lived for ever, he would be forever constituted as a lack of being seeking to fulfil himself in the future. Nonetheless, if he dies today then he has amounted, in the opinion of others, to what he is today and not to what he hoped to be in five years' time. In so far as death is the loss of a person's ability to influence the opinion of others as to the ultimate value of his life, anxiety in face of his being-towards-death is, not least, anxiety in face of others. Hence, he experiences anxiety over the fact that he may die before he has achieved success and proved himself to others, even though, presumably, to be dead is to have no awareness that posterity has labelled him a failure.

Finally, it is worth noting that even a toilet-cleaner who writes in his spare time and who eventually becomes a successful writer does not become a successful writer in the mode of being one. To repeat, the for-itself is constituted as a lack of being that can never be at one with the object of its desire. Considering the genius of Proust (*BN*, p. xxii; *EAH*, pp. 41–2), Sartre argues that even a genius cannot simply *be* a genius. Genius is as genius does. The genius of Proust is not an intrinsic quality of his being, but rather his literary achievements viewed as manifestations of his personality. This seems to suggest that, after all, a person is what he does, but this is not so. Although his actions and achievements shape his facticity, he has being only in so far as he perpetually transcends his facticity. To be is to do, but by doing a person does not become his being absolutely; his being is rather a constant becoming.

In further support of his claim that a person cannot be what he is in the mode of being it, Sartre explores the phenomenon of sadness.

OBJECTIFYING EMOTIONS – SADNESS

What Sartre says about sadness he holds to be true of any emotion, but by taking sadness as his example he avoids the confusion of considering an emotion such as anger that, though it is for consciousness, usually involves the Other. Admittedly, sadness often involves the Other, in so far as, for example, a lover is saddened by rejection, but it is far easier to make sense of the notion of feeling sad for no reason, of a sadness that is entirely a person's own affair, than it is to make sense of the notion of feeling angry for no reason. There is, for example, no difficulty in relating to Antonio's complaint with which Shakespeare opens *The Merchant of Venice*:

In sooth, I know not why I am so sad.
It wearies me; you say it wearies you;
But how I caught it, found it, or came by it,
What stuff 'tis made of, whereof it is born,
I am to learn;
(*The Merchant of Venice*, I, i)

The waiter strives playfully to be in himself what he is for others and what others make of him. Similarly, the sad person strives to be in himself what in actual fact he must make himself be. Initially, the claim that a sad person is not sad in the mode of being what he is is likely to meet with greater resistance than the claim that we are not identical with what we do. The fact that the waiter so evidently plays at being a waiter is sufficient to reveal that he is not really a waiter in the mode of being one. Surely though, if a person is sad then he is sad in the mode of being what he is; surely he is to be identified with his emotional state. To hold the view that a person is identical with his emotional state, however, is to fail to grasp that the for-itself is always other than itself and never self-identical. The nature of the for-itself implies that there is no such *thing* as an emotional state.

In everyday life it is not misleading to speak of a person being in a certain emotional state. When, in an everyday situation, a person behaving hysterically is described as being 'in an hysterical state', the intention is simply to convey an image of a distraught person who is screaming, crying and tearing at their hair. Many psychologists, however, are misled by such talk. Believing that mental and emotional phenomena have a certain objective existence they take the expression literally and go in search of the state of hysteria in itself – its psychological and physiological essence. But hysteria has no essence; hysteria is hysterical behaviour. Furthermore, what is true of temporary emotional states such as hysteria is also true of enduring mental conditions such as schizophrenia. Criticizing traditional psychology, R.D. Laing points out that having a mental condition such as schizophrenia is not like having a cold: 'No one *has* schizophrenia, like having a cold. The patient has not "got" schizophrenia. He is schizophrenic' (Laing 1990, p. 34). To define true madness, in contradiction to Shakespeare's Polonius: madness is never nothing else, but madness as a cold is nothing else but a cold.

Psychologists will object that many emotional states do have at least a physiological essence. Tourette's syndrome, for example, which is characterized by sudden, repetitive movements and utterances, is the result of certain neurochemical irregularities in the brain. However, that a person is subject by virtue of the facticity of his biology to involuntary spasms of aggressive behaviour, to a failure of aggression inhibition, does not mean that within his biology there exists the substantial being-in-itself of aggression. Although the Tourette's sufferer behaves aggressively due to physiological causes beyond his control, and is not therefore responsible for his actions, his aggression can no more be separated from his behaviour than a university can be separated from the buildings and functions that comprise it. Prior to the advancement of medical science, the Tourette's sufferer was thought to be possessed by aggression-in-itself – aggression personified as an evil spirit that existed independently of its manifestations. In reality, the Tourette's sufferer is no more possessed by aggression-in-itself than the buildings and functions of a university are possessed by the spirit of the university. To view aggression as something that can be separated from a person's aggressive behaviour is to make what Gilbert Ryle calls a category mistake. A category mistake involves misrepresenting the facts of mental life and placing them in the wrong logical category (Ryle 1990, p. 17).[9]

There is no such *thing* as sadness. The sad person is not a sad thing in the way that a ripe banana is a yellow thing. Sadness is rather the transcendent meaning of a certain set of gestures, a certain demeanour: 'It is the meaning of this dull look with which I view the world, of my bowed shoulders, of my lowered head, of the listlessness of my whole body' (*BN*, p. 61). As sadness is nothing but the meaning of these postures which a person must readopt moment by moment, he cannot take possession of his sadness. He can no more take possession of his sadness than he can take possession of himself (i.e., *be* himself in the mode of a for-itself-in-itself). Sadness is not a being but a conduct – the conduct of a person who makes himself sad (*BN*, p. 61). The requirement of having to be perpetually at a distance from himself in order to make himself sad means that he can never be sad in the mode of being what he is. 'If I make myself sad, it is because I am not sad – the being of the sadness escapes me by and in the very act by which I affect myself with it' (*BN*, p. 61). A person cannot give sadness to himself as he can give a gift to another. Precisely because he exists as that which strives to be being he cannot affect himself with being. In so far as his being is to be what he is not, he is sad only in so far as he makes himself sad and reflects upon himself as sad. His sadness is not an object in consciousness reflected on; it exists entirely in and through the act of reflection.

> If I make myself sad, I must continue to make myself sad from beginning to end. I can not treat my sadness as an impulse finally achieved and put it on file without recreating it, nor can I carry it in the manner of an inert body which continues its movement after the initial shock. There is no inertia in consciousness. (*BN*, p. 61)

I have argued that there is a sense in which the waiter is a waiter for the Other in a way that he cannot be a waiter for himself. Similarly, the sadness of another, especially when portrayed, appears to a person to have more substance than his own. As his sadness consists only in an irresolute commitment to be sad he may envy the sadness of others in so far as their sadness appears to him to be sadness in itself. He too would like to be the personification of sadness: a weeping, dejected god of melancholia pictured by an artist. Far from wanting to snap out of his sadness, he will want to honour a lost beloved with a sadness that is the quintessence of despair. Or, in bad faith, he will strive to become his sadness and despair in order to escape his freedom to hope that his beloved will return: a hope that tortures him with apprehension as it raises him up repeatedly only to cast him down. However, because sadness is only the conduct of a person who makes himself sad, he can never be, so to speak, sad enough.

The suffering which I experience, on the contrary, is never adequate suffering, due to the fact that it nihilates itself as in-itself by the very act by which it founds itself. It escapes as suffering towards the consciousness of suffering. I can never be *surprised* by it, for it *is* only to the exact degree that I experience it. Its translucency removes from it all depth. I can not observe it as I observe the suffering of the statue, since I make my own suffering and since I know it. If I must suffer, I should prefer that my suffering would seize me and flow over me like a storm, but instead I must raise it into existence in my free spontaneity. I should like simultaneously to be it and to conquer it, but this enormous, opaque suffering, which should transport me out of myself, continues instead to touch me lightly with its wings, and I can not grasp it. (*BN*, p. 92)

Sartre's analysis of sadness reveals the full extent to which, according to him, 'man is a useless passion' (*BN*, p. 615). Man is such a useless passion that he must despair even of becoming, as a last desperate means of escaping his free transcendence, a being in despair in the mode of being what he is. Sartre's position here echoes that of Søren Kierkegaard. In *The Sickness unto Death*, Kierkegaard considers a girl who despairs over the loss of her beloved: 'Just try now, just try saying to such a girl, "You are consuming yourself," and you will hear her answer, "O, but the torment is simply that I cannot do that"' (Kierkegaard 1989, p. 50) The girl has to be herself as despairing, rather than escape herself by having herself consumed by despair. She despairs of being at one with her despair as a means of escaping her consciousness of despair. She is in despair, as a consciousness of despair, because she can neither be her despair so as to escape her consciousness of it, nor escape her despair to become a happy being beyond despair. She cannot become a happy being beyond despair in the mode of being what she is because her being is to be what she is not and not to be what she is.

I see no grounds for challenging Sartre's view that sadness is not a ready-made being. He is right to insist that sadness, like hatred or any other emotion, is an intentional object for consciousness and that a person is sad only in so far as he is conscious of being sad. The notion that sadness is a thing in its own right separable from a person's consciousness of being sad is simply nonsensical. I also see no grounds for challenging Sartre's view that there is such a phenomenon as choosing to be sad. Life and art are full of sentimental characters that deliberately undertake to keep their melancholia alive as a last tentative link with a lost beloved. A will to sadness is evident on the part of people who prefer to wallow in self-pity rather than try to snap out of it. 'Grief is a species of idleness' (Johnson 1952). I do, however, see grounds for challenging Sartre's view that to be sad a person must always make himself sad, at least in so far as this view suggests that in every case a person can simply stop being sad if he chooses.

When criticizing Sartre's view of freedom earlier in this book I argued against Sartre that there appears to be a certain inertia in consciousness after all. This argument was supported by the evidence of various behavioural and dispositional phenomena that constitute limits to the capacity to choose. In light of these phenomena, Sartre's view regarding the relationship between choice and sadness (between choice and emotion generally) must be criticized.

Despite all that Sartre says to the contrary, it can be argued that there is sadness that is not chosen without thereby implying that sadness is a thing separable from a person's consciousness of being sad. Consider again Kierkegaard's example of the despairing girl. Accepting what has already been stated about the nature of her despair, any conscious attempt to escape her despair will confirm the very consciousness of despair she is seeking to escape. This is because in trying to be happy, she will remind herself that she is not happy. If her attempt to escape her sadness serves to confirm the very sadness she is seeking to escape, then sadness appears, contrary to Sartre's assertions, to have an inertia of its own.

Over time, however, people can escape a period of depression by changing their attitude and behaviour. If the depressed person depresses himself most by recalling how depressed he has been recently, then the solution is for him to strive to accumulate good memories. In this respect, Sartre is right to say that our emotions are subject to choice. We can make ourselves feel better over time by choosing to adopt a constructive pattern of behaviour. Unfortunately, the depressed person may well fear striving to cheer himself up because he fears his efforts will fail to cheer him up. Failure would reinforce his depression even more than simply not trying. A person who wants to be a winner may nonetheless avoid competing for fear of losing.

Even if Sartre conceded that people do not always make themselves sad, in the sense that they cannot instantly stop feeling sad, he would nonetheless argue that they make themselves sad initially. That is, a lover makes himself sad because he makes himself love. He chooses to be sad in so far as he chooses to be in love. This view is problematic.

Is it right simply to say that a lover chooses to be in love? Certainly, it makes sense to say that people choose to be in love, in so far as they adopt patterns of behaviour that reinforce their love rather than weaken it. Most people, however, have an unchosen propensity to form emotional attachments. They may choose the particular object of their desires, edifying and romanticizing their beloved so as to characterize them as all the more lovable, but they do not choose their desires. Earlier, I considered Merleau-Ponty's notion of the natural self – a notion that is absent from Sartre's thought. Arguably, the desire for sustained intimacy with another that is known as love belongs to this natural self. Rather than being something that is chosen, this desire is part of John Compton's pre-structure: 'the general background against which deliberate choices are made and personal histories develop' (Compton 1982, p. 585).

If it can be accepted that people do not choose to be in love – the popular view of love is that people fall in love despite themselves – then it can be accepted that in many cases people do not choose to be sad. Against Sartre, it can be argued that the sadness of a lover is the unavoidable consequence of an unsuccessful love affair. He does not make himself sad; he is made sad by the loss of something he was naturally predisposed to value. Of course, to say that his sadness is unavoidable is not to say that it is inescapable. Like any other sad or depressed person he has the potential to reinvent himself over time as a being beyond his current misery. Reinvention, however, will involve forming new attachments to people, places, possessions and projects that may fail him in various ways. The threat of falling victim to further unchosen sadness remains.

Even if it is accepted, as Sartre argues, that a lover makes himself love, that his love is entirely chosen, it does not follow that a lover chooses to be sad because he chooses to be in love. Certainly, if he chooses to be in love he is laying himself open to the risk of sadness, but this is not the same as saying that he chooses to be sad, or that he makes himself sad. It can only be said that he chooses sadness by choosing love if sadness is an inevitable consequence of love and he is aware that it is an inevitable consequence. But sadness is surely not an inevitable consequence of love, despite what the cynics say.

Arguably, people do not choose all the emotional consequences of their choices. Indeed, the choice of a particular course of action tends to determine the emotional states that arise thereafter. If a person chooses to do work that demands intense and sustained concentration, for example, then it is inevitable that he will be irritated by constant interruptions to his work. Certainly, he can undertake not to be irritated, but this would involve choosing not to work rather than simply choosing not to be irritated. Although he does not choose to be irritated, he must, however, take responsibility for the fact that he is irritated. He would, for example, be in bad faith if he blamed others for his irritation, especially if they were not trying deliberately to interrupt him. After all, constant interruptions to his work would not be felt by him to be irritating if he was not disposed by his choice of work to be irritated. The unchosen irritation that arises within him as an inevitable consequence of previous choices belongs to his facticity. As soon as the irritation arises he must, as with all facticity, choose his response to it. It is in this sense that he is responsible for it. He is not directly responsible for generating it but he is responsible for how he deals with it.

The above account applies to a sane adult in ordinary, everyday circumstances. It is not applicable, however, to an insane person, or to a young child, or to a person whose emotional state is so extreme that it gives rise directly to reflexive behaviour that does not involve his will. As noted, extreme panic, for example, can overwhelm consciousness, giving rise to a fight-or-flight reaction over which a person, though he remains starkly conscious, has no control. Once again, the conclusion to be drawn is that Sartre is right to argue that people are often far more responsible for their feelings and actions than they tend to realize or admit, but that he is wrong to argue that everyone is always responsible for their feelings and actions.

INSINCERITY AND SINCERITY: THE HOMOSEXUAL AND THE CHAMPION OF SINCERITY

A person can try to be sincere, he can believe that he is sincere, he can hold that he is what he is and declare 'I am what I am', but he cannot *be* sincere. Sincerity is unachievable because, as noted, it is impossible for a person to be what he is. 'The original structure of "not being what one is" renders impossible in advance all movement towards being in itself or "being what one is" ' (*BN*, p. 62). Far from being a project in good faith, as might be supposed, the project of sincerity is in bad faith. To attempt to be sincere and say, 'I am what I am', is to attempt to deny that the for-itself is transcendent and never what it is but always what it is not and not what it is. Arguing that sincerity is as much a phenomenon of bad faith as insincerity, Sartre offers the example of the homosexual and the champion of sincerity (*BN*, pp. 63–5). These two characters also serve to highlight two further aspects of bad faith: the bad faith involved in stereotyping others and the bad faith involved in the act of confession.

Drawing upon an episode from his own experience that he mentions in a letter to Simone de Beauvoir (*LC*, pp. 142–3), Sartre describes a homosexual who, plagued by feelings of guilt, denies that he is a homosexual (*BN*, p. 63). His denial does not involve a refusal to recognize his homosexual desires or even a disavowal of his homosexual activities. As argued, such a deliberate and cynical attempt at self-deception would fail completely. Rather, his denial involves a refusal to recognize homosexuality as the transcendent meaning of his conduct. Like the person who is in the habit of listening at doors (*BN*, pp. 259–60), he chooses, in bad faith, to characterize his conduct as a series of aberrations.

> His case is always 'different', peculiar; there enters into it something of a game, of chance, of bad luck; the mistakes are all in the past; they are explained by a certain conception of the beautiful which women can not satisfy; we should see in them the result of a restless search, rather than the manifestations of a deeply rooted tendency, etc., etc. Here is assuredly a man in bad faith who borders on the comic since, acknowledging all the facts which are imputed to him, he refuses to draw from them the conclusion which they impose. (*BN*, p. 63)

How does the homosexual sustain this duplicity? The answer is that he believes a homosexual is not a homosexual in the mode of being one: that a homosexual is not a homosexual as a table is a table. This belief is justified. Like the waiter, the lecturer or the sad person, the homosexual is not a homosexual in the sense that a table is a table because it is impossible for a person simply to be what they are. The homosexual is, however, a homosexual in the mode of being what he is not. He is a homosexual in so far as homosexuality is the transcendent meaning of his conduct. It is this fact that the homosexual avoids facing. His avoidance of this fact is achieved by playing upon the meaning of the verb 'to be'. He is not a homosexual in the mode of being one, but he takes this to imply that he is not a homosexual in the mode of not being what he is not, when in fact he is a homosexual in the mode of being what he is not.

> he plays on the word *being*. He would be right actually if he understood the phrase, 'I am not a paederast' in the sense of 'I am not what I am.' That is, if he declared to himself, 'To the extent that a pattern of conduct is defined as the conduct of a paederast and to the extent that I have adopted this conduct, I am a paederast. But to the extent that human reality can not be finally defined by patterns of conduct I am not one.' But instead he slides surreptitiously towards a different connotation of the word 'being'. He understands 'not being' in the sense of 'not-being-in-itself'. He lays claim to 'not being a paederast' in the sense in which this table is not an inkwell. He is in bad faith. (*BN*, p. 64)[10]

To make the point in terms of facticity and temporal transcendence, the homosexual attempts to deny that he is his facticity, when in fact he is his facticity in the mode of not being it: in the mode of no longer being it. That is, though he is not his facticity – his past – in the mode of being it, he is nonetheless his facticity in so far as it is the past being which he affirms as belonging to him by virtue of the fact that he must continually surpass and transcend it towards the future. He assumes in bad faith that he is a pure transcendence, that his facticity, being past, has dissolved into the absolute nothingness of a generalized past. The truth of the matter, however, is that far from being a pure transcendence he is and must be the transcendence of his facticity. Facticity and transcendence are locked in an original synthesis. The homosexual, in his project of bad faith, attempts to deny this synthesis and create within himself a divide between facticity and transcendence. As Anthony Manser points out in 'A new look at bad faith', this creation of a divide between facticity and transcendence also characterizes the project of sincerity championed by the homosexual's friend (Manser 1987).

The homosexual has a friend, a 'champion of sincerity' (*BN*, p. 63). He is irritated by the homosexual's continued refusal to recognize what he is. He urges him to declare himself and admit that he is a homosexual. Sartre asks which one is in bad faith, the homosexual or the champion of sincerity? (*BN*, p. 63). The answer seems obvious. The homosexual is in bad faith because of his duplicity, whereas the champion of sincerity, as an advocate of honesty, is in good faith. This, however, is not the case. The right answer is that the champion of sincerity is as much in bad faith as his homosexual friend. Why is this?

In encouraging the homosexual to be sincere about his homosexuality the champion of sincerity encourages him to constitute himself as a thing: to be just a homosexual. He offers to relieve him of his freedom as freedom and to return it to him as a thing; to exchange a limitless freedom for a freedom reduced to a fixed and known quantity. Although this offer of relief purports to be entirely altruistic in that it offers the homosexual an escape from the burden of his freedom, the champion of sincerity actually has a selfish motive. He finds it reassuring to reduce the homosexual to a thing because as a thing the homosexual ceases to be a transcendent freedom with the power to negate the transcendent freedom of others. In persuading the homosexual to accept a definition the champion of sincerity gains power over him. The homosexual ceases to be a limitless and threatening freedom and becomes instead a fixed and known quantity. He is labelled 'homosexual' and is nothing more; he is pigeon-holed and explained away like the old crackpot in *Nausea*: 'He [Dr Rogé] looks at the little man with his fierce eyes. A direct gaze which puts everything in its place. He explains: "He's an old crackpot, that's what he is" ' (*N*, p. 99).

Dr Rogé stereotypes the little man; the champion of sincerity stereotypes the homosexual. To stereotype a person is to deny that he is free to transcend definitions; it is to deny that he has a dimension of individuality that makes him more than simply a member of a particular race, class or religious group. The champion of sincerity is in bad faith because the real aim of his call for sincerity is to escape his own anxieties by attempting to constitute the transcendence of the homosexual as a facticity.[11] 'The champion of sincerity is in bad faith to the degree that in order to reassure himself, he pretends to judge, to the extent that he demands that freedom *as* freedom constitute itself as a thing' (*BN*, p. 65).

The key point here is that a person is as much in bad faith when he seeks to affirm the transcendence of the Other as facticity and vice versa, as when he seeks to affirm his own transcendence as facticity and vice versa. Recalling the example of the flirt (*BN*, p. 55), it can be seen that one aspect of her bad faith involves treating the transcendent freedom of the Other as though it were a facticity. Specifically, she refuses to acknowledge the transcendent meaning of the words and gestures of her suitor.

The champion of sincerity reassures himself by reducing the homosexual to a thing. It is possible that the homosexual would also find this reduction reassuring. Intolerable feelings of guilt cause the homosexual to fear accepting himself as a homosexual, yet surprisingly, choosing the sincerity championed by his friend would be a means of escaping these feelings of guilt. Sincerity can protect a person against himself by allowing him to escape his guilt and anguish through the divorce of his own past being. Sincerity appears to be a simple act of honesty in which a person accepts what he is, but the sincere person is in bad faith because the real aim of his sincerity is actually to distance himself from what he is through the very act by which he accepts what he is. 'The essential structure of sincerity does not differ from that of bad faith since the sincere man constitutes himself as what he is *in order not to be it*' (*BN*, p. 65). To clarify what Sartre means by this it is necessary to compare good and bad faith and to give an account of sincerity in terms of facticity and transcendence.

'Sincerity' is usually defined as 'good faith' and 'insincerity' as 'bad faith'. For Sartre, however, good faith and bad faith, far from being opposites, are ontologically identical. In his view, the fact that bad faith is a peculiar and subtle form of dishonesty does not mean that good faith, by contrast, is a form of honesty. Good faith is a project of dishonesty that has the same underlying structure as bad faith. Good faith is a project in bad faith. That is, good faith is bad faith in that they are fundamentally the same project. Good faith, or the project of sincerity, is bad faith because sincerity, like every other project of bad faith, exploits the double property of the person as both a facticity and a transcendence. The homosexual attempts to create a gulf between his facticity and his transcendence. He denies that he is his facticity in the mode of not being it in order to constitute himself as a pure transcendence. A sincere person also attempts to create a gulf between his facticity and his transcendence so as to constitute himself as a pure transcendence, except that his approach is to affirm that he is his facticity in the mode of being it so as to immediately escape being it by virtue of that very affirmation. The sincere person declares that he is a thing in order immediately to distance himself from the thing that he declares himself to be. In declaring that he is a thing he is no longer a thing but rather that which declares he is a thing.

> Total, constant sincerity as a constant effort to adhere to oneself is by nature a constant effort to dissociate oneself from oneself. A person frees himself from himself by the very act by which he makes himself an object for himself. To draw up a perpetual inventory of what one is means constantly to redeny oneself and to take refuge in a sphere where one is no longer anything but a pure, free regard. The goal of bad faith . . . is to put oneself out of reach; it is an escape. (*BN*, p. 65)

Sincerity is a project of escape. This is best revealed by looking at the phenomenon of confession. Sartre considers the example of the man who confesses he is evil (*BN*, p. 65). In confessing his evil, 'he has exchanged his disturbing "freedom-for-evil" for an inanimate character of evil' (*BN*, p. 65). It is as though his confession renders his evil into an inanimate psychic object for his contemplation; an evil that exists only in so far as he contemplates it and ceases to exist when he ceases to contemplate it. 'He escapes from that *thing*, since it is he who contemplates it, since it depends on him to maintain it under his glance or to let it collapse in an infinity of particular acts' (*BN*, p. 65). Believing himself to be a pure transcendence he believes he is free to move on from his evil and to abandon it to the past as a disarmed evil that is neither his possession nor his responsibility. He tells himself, 'my future is virgin; everything is allowed to me' (*BN*, p. 65).

Exposing sincerity as a form of escape explains why a sin confessed is a sin half pardoned. Confession, far from being an acceptance of guilt and responsibility, is a subtle means of rejecting them. A person who confesses to a priest, for example, deliberately aims to rid himself of guilt, although in bad faith he will avoid admitting to himself that this is his motive. In confessing his misdeeds to a priest a person makes himself an object for the priest. His sense of guilt, in truth the result of a freely chosen attitude towards past thoughts and deeds, appears as an object also. His sense of guilt becomes a state of sin. As guilt in-itself this state of sin can be spirited away by forgiveness; it can be removed and destroyed like waste. Priests are effective dustmen of the soul.

A person may even expect his sincerity to be praised. Sartre argues that the person who confesses he is evil does so in order to gain credit for superseding his evilness by his act of confession (*BN*, p. 65). Echoing Sartre's point, Joseph Catalano considers people who confess to the vice of laziness:

> Our sincerity appears as honesty but it is an honesty that points away from our laziness and calls attention to our virtue of honesty. This apparent honesty is a subtle way of letting our [vices] remain intact. It is a way of praising ourselves for our apparent self-knowledge. We see our sincerity as an ideal position from which we objectively judge our vices. What we do not admit is that our sincerity is also open to question because it is only a partial view of ourselves. (Catalano 1993, p. 81)[12]

Confession in both religious and secular contexts provides an effective means of escaping feelings of guilt. It is not surprising, therefore, that the guilty are often driven by a need to confess. The need to confess is a recurrent theme in the novels of Dostoevsky. For the sake of their peace of mind several of Dostoevsky's characters eventually own up to their crimes. Such a character is the Mysterious Visitor in *The Brothers Karamazov*. His story is told by Father Zossima to Alexey Karamazov.

> He told me he had been thinking of killing himself. But instead of that, he became obsessed by another dream, a dream which he considered insane and impossible at first, but which finally gripped his heart so strongly that he could not shake it off. He dreamed of getting up, going out before the people and publicly confessing that he had committed a murder. For three years he nurtured that dream in his heart and he thought of all sorts of ways of carrying it out. At last he believed with all his heart that by making a public confession of his crime, he would most certainly restore his peace of mind and set it at rest once and for all. (Dostoevsky 1958, pp. 361–2)

Dostoevsky undoubtedly recognizes and marvels at the power of confession to effect a break with the past and bring about a quantum leap into a virgin future. It is far less certain, however, that he recognizes confession as being in bad faith. On the contrary, being of the opinion that genuine good faith is possible, he considers confession to be an act of good faith. He even views the power of confession to dispel guilt as miraculous. For him, the moment of confession is a moment of divine intervention. There is not simply, as Sartre argues, the illusion of having sins taken away and past misdeeds effaced as though they had never happened, but a genuine rebirth of innocence.

It can be asked why, if there is divine intervention, a person must give his confession to another person to be relieved of his guilt? Why can't he simply pray to God to take his guilt away? Dostoevsky might reply that God only grants forgiveness to a person and takes his guilt away when the person has achieved a new level of awareness and respect for others that he lacked when he was in the habit of wronging them. The act of confession, because it involves a person baring his soul before others and exposing himself to the opinion of others, signifies that this new level of awareness and respect for others has been achieved. This would appear to be the case with Raskolnikov, the hero of Dostoevsky's *Crime and Punishment*.

Through guilt – which is its own punishment – and finally confession, Raskolnikov discovers a new-found love and respect for others that he lacked as a malicious egoist. In truly acknowledging other people, especially his lover Sonia, he is able to accept their love and forgiveness and in turn love and forgive himself. For Dostoevsky, this is a divine mystery comparable to the Christian miracle of rebirth and resurrection.

> He had come back to life, and he knew it, and felt it, with every fibre of his renewed being . . . And what did all, *all* the torments of the past amount to now? Everything, even his crime, even his sentence and punishment appeared to him now, in the first transport of feeling, a strange extraneous event that did not seem even to have happened to him. (Dostoevsky 1951, p. 558)

Has Raskolnikov undergone spiritual rebirth or has he simply fallen into bad faith? Clearly, within the context of the novel he has undergone spiritual rebirth. In real life, however, is spiritual rebirth possible? Despite arguing that it is bad faith for a person to strive to divorce his former self, Sartre, perhaps surprisingly, suggests the possibility of radical conversion to authentic being – an existential form of rebirth. A detailed exploration of authenticity and its relationship to bad faith forms the subject matter of the final part of this book. There I will look again at the character of Raskolnikov and attempt to answer the question concerning the possibility of spiritual rebirth. At present, it remains to consider Sartre's final example of a character in bad faith.

BEING AND NOT BEING WHAT WE ARE – THE COWARD

Sartre's final example of a character in bad faith is that of the coward who seeks to consider himself as not being cowardly (*BN*, pp. 66–7). In so far as a person is never what he is in the mode of being it, the coward is not a coward in the mode of an object, even if the transcendent meaning of his behaviour is that he is a coward. The fact that he is not a coward in the mode of being one allows him to call his cowardice into question and to slide surreptitiously into the false assumption that he is not a coward in the mode of not being what he is not. In this respect he is no different from the homosexual who undertakes in bad faith to deny that he is his past in the mode of not being it by affirming the falsehood that he is not his past in the mode of not being it (*BN*, pp. 63–4).

The example of the coward does not simply cover old ground, it allows Sartre to summarize his position regarding sincerity and bad faith and to form general conclusions. His main conclusion is that the ever-present possibility of bad faith implies that the being of the for-itself is to be what it is not and not to be what it is. The chapter on bad faith appears early on in *Being and Nothingness*, before the chapter on the immediate structures of the for-itself, at a point where Sartre is still introducing the notion that the being of the for-itself is to be what it is not and not to be what it is. He explores bad faith not only for its own sake but as a means of providing evidence for his view that the for-itself lacks self-identity. Bad faith would be impossible if the for-itself were self-identical. The existence of bad faith implies that the for-itself is as Sartre describes it. 'The condition of the possibility of bad faith is that human reality, in its most immediate being, in the intra-structure of the pre-reflective cogito, must be what it is not and not be what it is' (*BN*, p. 67).

If the for-itself was identical with itself then it would be impossible for the coward to strive to deny the meaning of his behaviour by appealing to his free transcendence. If he was an in-itself, as a table is a table, then he would have no free transcendence to appeal to. Similarly, if the for-itself was identical with itself then the sincere person could not posit himself as x in order to escape himself as x. If he was identical with himself as x he could not even posit himself as x, he would simply be x. To posit himself as x requires that he be at a distance from himself in order to be able to represent himself to himself. The fact that a person is always at a distance from himself, however, does not imply that he can completely escape himself (his former self). It has been argued repeatedly that a person is the transcendence of his facticity, not a pure transcendence in itself. If transcendence meant complete escape from facticity, a person would have no choice but to be reborn as a completely new self, moment by moment. This would amount to the complete disintegration of the self as a coherent and ongoing process of becoming. Instead of being a for-itself constituted as the ongoing transcendence of facticity, a person would be a series of in-itselves linked by nothing but a series of moments of transcendence (i.e., not transcendence as ongoing transcendence of facticity, but transcendence as repeated detachment from facticity). As transcendence is transcendence of facticity, however, and nothing beyond that, the notion that transcendence can somehow detach itself from facticity is nonsensical. As a project of escape, sincerity cannot really achieve its goal any more than a man can grasp his shadow in order to cast it away.

CHAPTER 6

THE FAITH OF BAD FAITH – THE PRIMITIVE PROJECT

> This original project of bad faith is a decision in bad faith on the nature of faith.
>
> (*BN*, p. 68)

For a proper understanding of bad faith it is vital to understand the faith of bad faith (*BN*, p. 67). Bad faith makes sense only if an explanation can be given of how a person sustains particular projects of bad faith against the imminent threat of realizing that he is in bad faith. Realizing that he is in bad faith would undermine his particular projects of bad faith by exposing them as states of false consciousness in which he believes in himself as a being-in-itself. It can be argued that it is impossible for a person to be in bad faith because he cannot undertake to be in bad faith without realizing he is doing so. Arguably, false consciousness is unachievable because it is impossible for a person to make a deliberate shift from an authentic attitude in which he affirms his transcendence to an attitude in which he attempts to identify himself with the in-itself. In answering this objection, Sartre argues that in order to succeed, 'the project of bad faith must be itself in bad faith' (*BN*, pp. 67–8). He argues that although people choose their particular projects of bad faith, they do not choose to be in bad faith as such. Rather, they are already in bad faith in the form of a primitive project of bad faith (*BN*, p. 68) that predisposes them towards particular projects of bad faith. People do not deliberately undertake the primitive project of bad faith, they fall into it, like falling asleep. 'Let us understand clearly that there is no question of a reflective, voluntary decision, but of a spontaneous determination of our being. One puts oneself in bad faith as one goes to sleep and one is in bad faith as one dreams.' (*BN*, p. 68).

The second sentence of the above remark is misleading. If falling into bad faith is like falling asleep, then a person does not put himself in bad faith any more than he puts himself to sleep. He decides to go to bed and to put himself in the way of sleep by adopting a relaxed position and calming his thoughts, but he falls asleep when he is overcome by sleep. If Sartre simply meant to say that falling into bad faith is like falling asleep then this would sit more comfortably with the first part of his remark as well as with remarks that he makes elsewhere about the primitive project of bad faith. To say that a person puts himself in bad faith implies that he knows he has done so. It does not meet the objection that bad faith is impossible that Sartre wants to refute. To say, however, that falling into bad faith is like falling asleep and that no decision is involved meets the objection. That is, it cannot be objected that bad faith is impossible because people cannot undertake to be in it, if the truth of the matter is that people do not undertake to be in bad faith.

If being in bad faith in the primitive mode of being generally predisposed towards particular projects of bad faith is like being asleep, then a person in bad faith cannot recall having fallen into bad faith and no more recognizes that he is in bad faith than he recognizes that he is asleep. It may even be the case that a person falls into the faith of bad faith at the first moment of self-consciousness. That is, at the moment when, as a child, he first discovers himself as a being in the world upon which he can take a point of view, he immediately reacts by identifying himself exclusively with his objective mode of being. In discovering that he is a thing for others, he assumes that he is also a thing for himself. What is the motivation for this reaction?

Arguably, when a child comes to self-consciousness he is immediately motivated to see himself as a thing having a definite, determined existence. In this way he escapes the anguish he would experience if he saw himself as an indeterminate and superfluous freedom adrift in a world of terrible possibilities. Echoing Kierkegaard, Sartre notes that anguish and fear are different (*BN*, p. 29). A person's fear is his concern for his determinate, objective self – his body – whereas his anguish is his concern over his indeterminacy and the fact that he must constantly determine himself. Sartre clarifies the distinction between anguish and fear in the following passage:

> Vertigo is anguish to the extent that I am afraid not of falling over the precipice, but of throwing myself over. A situation provokes

fear if there is a possibility of my life being changed from without; my being provokes anguish to the extent that I distrust myself and my own reactions to that situation. (*BN*, p. 29)

In this case the person employs various strategies to avoid his sense of anguish. In attempting to ignore his freedom to jump over the precipice he absorbs himself in the task of carefully picking his way along the path as though it were the demands of the situation that determined his actions rather than himself. He imagines himself subject to psychological determinism and compelled to act in accordance with survival instinct. The motive of survival is presumed to have the power to determine his actions, but in truth it has only the significance he chooses to give it. His project is to affirm facticity as transcendence and transcendence as facticity, a project that, as noted, lies at the heart of bad faith.

The example of the precipice-walker shows how bad faith can protect a person's physical well-being. Bad faith can also protect a person's social standing from dangerous experiments in freedom.

A young bride was in terror, when her husband left her alone, of sitting in the window and summoning passers-by like a prostitute. Nothing in her education, in her past, nor in her character could serve as an explanation of such a fear. It seems to us simply that a negligible circumstance (reading, conversation, etc.) had determined in her what might be called a 'vertigo of possibility'. She found herself monstrously free, and this vertiginous freedom appeared to her *at the opportunity* for this action which she was afraid of doing. (*TE*, p. 100)

The young bride is in need of bad faith to prevent her from succumbing to the vertigo of possibility and to spare her the anguish of even contemplating acting with impropriety. Bad faith can protect the psychological well-being of a person by serving as a guard rail against anguish. This in turn is good for a person's physical well-being because anguish, as a form of stress, is unhealthy.

On the other hand, there are cases where bad faith does not contribute to a person's well-being. Bad faith can, for example, sustain a debilitating phobia. Arguably, a phobia can be conquered by overcoming the bad faith within which it functions. Achieving an intellectual awareness of bad faith can be the first step towards a person conquering his arachnophobia, for example. Realizing that he cannot be a person who fears spiders in the mode of being what he is, he will realize that he must be choosing himself, in bad faith, as a person who has no choice but to fear spiders: a choice that he reaffirms every time he reacts in fear of them. The solution to the phobia is for him to refrain by an act of will from all behaviour (killing spiders, running from them, and so on) that reinforces his false belief that his fear is a thing; a possession that determines his responses. Eventually, he will expose his fear as nothing but a self-perpetuating project of fear that he has abandoned by changing his behaviour.

That it would be advantageous for a person to overcome certain projects of bad faith does not imply that it would be advantageous for him to overcome bad faith completely. Particular disadvantages of bad faith must be weighed against overall advantages. A person who, for example, is hampered and repressed in some respects by neuroses maintained in bad faith, would not necessarily gain by overcoming these neuroses. His neurotic behaviour might be a more or less harmless means of dissipating anguish that would otherwise cause him a mental breakdown. In this case, as in the case of the precipice-walker, bad faith can be seen as a coping strategy. Neurotic behaviour might even be the key to a person's success if it disposes him towards organization in his life and perfectionism in his work.

Not only does bad faith provide a means of averting the perhaps unbearable anguish that results from a full awareness of freedom, it also provides a means of relieving unbearable guilt. As noted, bad faith in the form of sincerity enables a person to escape his guilt-ridden self via the act of confession. In Nietzsche's opinion – I shall consider his position more closely in due course – it is cowardly and ignoble for a person to seek to divorce his former self. Nonetheless, the fact remains that confession contributes to the sense of well-being of ordinary people like Dostoevsky's Raskolnikov who lack the incredible strength of character required 'To redeem the past and to transform every "it was" into "thus I willed it"' (Nietzsche 1988, p. 161).

Bad faith may well be far more than just a coping strategy. Arguably, it is a vital element of each person's psychological make-up. If a person did not to some extent commit himself to a belief in himself as a certain kind of person with a given character he would not know who he was from one situation to the next. He would always be a stranger to himself and to others. Such a person, a person who did not consider himself to be a kind of thing, or who did not at least play at being a kind of thing with faith in his performance, would be insane. For example, Roquentin, the hero of Sartre's novel *Nausea*, is a man who has lost faith in himself as a particular character. He no longer believes in his own performance, and as a result his life has a 'halting, incoherent aspect' (*N*, p. 14). He strives to live according to the existential truth that his existence is absurd, contingent and without foundation, and in so doing he exhibits markedly psychotic tendencies.

The implications are that without bad faith, at least at the level of a primitive project, a person's character lacks coherence. The primitive project of bad faith is like the bad faith of Sartre's waiter who plays with great conviction at being a waiter. I have argued that the bad faith of the waiter is not bad faith in the strict sense because his aim is to be at one with his performance rather than to become a waiter-thing. The waiter's attitude is one of belief in his performance: belief in the form of a suspension of disbelief. Almost exactly the same can be said of the primitive project of bad faith. The primitive project of bad faith involves a person suspending his disbelief in his belief in himself. It is a fundamental commitment not to disbelieve belief, nor to question it too closely. Not least, it is a commitment committed to not questioning or doubting itself. 'Bad faith in its primitive project and in its coming into the world decides on the exact nature of its requirements. It stands forth in the firm resolution *not to demand too much*, to count itself satisfied when it is barely persuaded, to force itself in decisions to adhere to uncertain truths' (*BN*, p. 68).

It is illuminating to compare Sartre's idea of the primitive project of bad faith with the idea of not spelling-out put forward by Herbert Fingarette in *Self-Deception*. Fingarette argues that to be conscious of doing something is not necessarily to be explicitly conscious of doing it. Indeed, on most occasions a person does not spell-out to himself what he is doing.[1] That is, in doing *x* he does not generally reflect upon the fact that he is doing *x*, either in the form of contemplating himself from the point of view of others or in the form of a commentary upon what he is doing. 'When I ride a bicycle, drive a car, form and utter sentences in English, dress myself, play the violin, sit down in a chair, walk, handle my body, I usually exercise these skills well, at times with art; yet most of the time I do not spell-out, not even to myself, what I am doing' (Fingarette 2000, pp. 41–2).[2] Fingarette goes on to argue that not spelling-out in particular cases is sustained by a general policy of not spelling-out, which is not itself spelt-out. 'The *policy* of not spelling-out . . . is a "self-covering" policy. To adopt it is, perforce, never to make it explicit, to "hide" it.' (Fingarette 2000, p. 49). Arguably, the self-covering policy of not spelling-out is identical to the primitive project of bad faith. Just as particular projects of bad faith are sustained by a primitive project of bad faith that prevents a person from recognizing that he is in bad faith, so particular failures to spell-out are sustained by a general policy of not spelling-out that is not itself spelt-out. Whereas Fingarette refers to a person not spelling-out his general policy of not spelling-out, Sartre refers to a person not believing that a belief is a belief. If a person comes to believe that a belief is a belief he will recognize it for what it is, a mere belief, and no longer wholeheartedly believe it. 'To believe is to know that one believes, and to know that one believes is no longer to believe . . . Every belief is a belief that falls short; one never wholly believes what one believes' (*BN*, p. 69). A person is able to suspend disbelief in a belief because he fails to spell-out to himself the fact that a belief is merely a belief. Spelling-out the policy of not spelling-out undermines the policy. Coming to believe that a belief is merely a belief undermines the belief. If a person comes to believe that a belief is a belief then he ceases to be convinced by it and loses faith in it, because, by its very nature, belief implies doubt.

In arguing that belief implies doubt Wittgenstein notes that the expression, 'I believed' always means 'I no longer believe'. It follows, therefore, that ' "I believe" can't *properly* be the present of "I believed" ' (Wittgenstein 1980, 700). A proper present tense of 'I believed' would have to express lack of belief. 'I believe' does not express lack of belief, although it does express a measure of doubt. If a person says, for example, 'I believe in the existence of God', then it is because he is not certain of the existence of God. If God's existence was certain, it would be as strange to say, 'I believe in the existence of God', as it would be to say, 'I believe in the existence of chairs', the existence of which (extreme scepticism aside) is certain. Belief is an attitude that is only relevant when a person is uncertain. He can believe what he does not know for certain, but he does not also believe what he knows for certain, even if it is impossible for him to disbelieve what he knows for certain. That a person cannot disbelieve what he knows does not mean that he believes what he knows. He does not believe what he knows, he knows it. 'I believe' is redundant when a person is speaking of matters about which he is certain.

This is not to say that to refrain from talk of belief is to be certain, but rather that to talk meaningfully of belief is to reveal uncertainty, even if the use of 'I believe' is often intended to 'indicate the unwavering firmness of belief' (*BN*, p. 69). Beliefs can be firm, they can be strongly and widely held and frequently expressed, but because they are beliefs they are always uncertain.[3]

Having gained various insights into the nature of the primitive project of bad faith, it is worth returning again to the question of the very possibility of bad faith; the question of how a person sustains particular projects of bad faith against the imminent threat of realizing that he is in bad faith. If, as suggested, to emerge into self-consciousness is inevitably to fall into a primitive project of bad faith that averts overwhelming anguish and maintains sanity, then here is another way of meeting the objection that bad faith is impossible because it is impossible to make a deliberate shift to false consciousness. If self-consciousness always emerges in a state of bad faith then it never shifts from authenticity to bad faith, but only from bad faith to authenticity. This implies that authenticity is not an original way of being from which there is a decline into bad faith, but rather that authenticity is a way of being that must be obtained through an overcoming of bad faith. This is not to say that bad faith is an original way of being, but rather that there is a fall into bad faith from a state of non-reflective innocence that is not characterized by bad faith or by authenticity. Babies and young children are authentic in the sense that they are genuine and do not have a false view of themselves, but they are not authentic in Sartre's sense of being self-responsible people for whom freedom is the ultimate value. I will now explore Sartre's view of authenticity in detail.

PART 4

AUTHENTICITY

CHAPTER 7

SARTRE ON AUTHENTICITY

What I also learnt – and I note it down here without further elabora-
tion – is that it's much easier to live decently and authentically in
wartime than in peacetime.

(*WD*, p. 197)

Of all Sartre's central themes his notion of authenticity is the most
difficult to clarify. Nowhere does he provide an account of authenticity as detailed as his accounts of consciousness, freedom and bad
faith. In *Being and Nothingness* he makes scant reference to the phenomenon and has nothing to say by way of explanation. He only hints
at the possibility of a radical conversion to authentic being, merely
suggesting that people need not live in bad faith. Furthermore, the
promise he makes at the close of *Being and Nothingness* to explore the
issue of authenticity in a later work was never completely fulfilled. He
often expressed an intention to provide a detailed account of authenticity, but he never succeeded in providing more than a sketchy outline
of the phenomenon. He certainly never fulfilled the prediction of a
friend who wrote to him in 1939 declaring, 'you'll shortly be writing
a wonderful book in several volumes on authenticity' (*WD*, p. 61).

Nonetheless, Sartre says enough on the subject of authenticity in
various places, both directly and indirectly, to allow his insights to
be developed in ways that remain true to the guiding principles of
his existentialism. It is partly because Sartre's account of authenticity demands this development that scholars find it so fascinating.
Here, perhaps more than in any other area of his philosophy, Sartre
challenges posterity to carry on where he left off.

The best way to begin developing an account of Sartre's view
of authenticity is to consider what authenticity is not. That is, to

consider Sartre's account of inauthentic being. If one thing can be said with certainty about Sartre's account of authenticity it is that he holds authenticity to be the antithesis of bad faith. Bad faith is synonymous with inauthenticity. More specifically, it is certain that he holds authenticity to be distinct from sincerity; sincerity being a mode of bad faith. In order to develop an account of authenticity as the antithesis of inauthenticity it is necessary to revisit Sartre's examples of people in bad faith and highlight the main features of their inauthenticity. Sartre's examples of people in bad faith reveal that the most blatant feature of inauthenticity is the attempted evasion of responsibility. Sartre's flirt (*BN*, pp. 55–6) attempts to avoid taking responsibility for her present situation, while Sartre's homosexual and the champion of sincerity (*BN*, pp. 63–5) attempt to avoid, in their different ways, taking responsibility for their past deeds.

Sartre's flirt represents inauthentic people who attempt to avoid taking responsibility for their actions by choosing not to choose. Such people, by choosing to suppose that they have no choice, exercise their freedom in a self-defeating manner. They choose to suppose that they cannot do or be otherwise and that they have no option to change. They attempt to make themselves synonymous with the in-itself.

Sartre's homosexual represents inauthentic people who, having realized the truth that there is nothing that they are in the mode of being it, attempt to avoid taking responsibility for their past deeds by declaring that they are not their past in the sense that a table is not a chair. Recall Sartre's argument that although the homosexual is not his past – his facticity – in the mode of being it, he is nonetheless his facticity in so far as he affirms it as belonging to him by virtue of the fact that he must continually transcend it towards the future. Sartre's homosexual, despite endorsing the truth that there is nothing that he is in the mode of being it, assumes that he is his transcendence in the mode of being it by denying that he is the transcendence of his facticity.

Finally, the champion of sincerity represents inauthentic people who attempt to avoid taking responsibility for what they are by declaring, 'I am what I am.' Prima facie, it appears that people who make such a declaration are taking full responsibility for themselves, but a closer examination reveals that this is not so. In declaring, 'I am what I am', sincere people are saying, 'I cannot help what I am – what I do.' Rather than view their actions as the expression of their choices they view them as though they are caused phenomena determined by an inner nature or essence for which they are not responsible. Like people who choose not to choose, they also attempt to make themselves synonymous with the in-itself. Sartre's account of sincerity, however, is more involved than this. Although he would not deny the existence of the simple sincerity just described, in his view the project of sincerity tends to be more sophisticated, involving a more cunning project in which a person constitutes himself as what he is in order not to be it. Recall Sartre's argument that sincerity is a project of escape. In constituting himself as an object that he contemplates, the champion of sincerity distances himself from that object by the very fact that he contemplates it. He identifies himself wholly with that which contemplates what he declares to be his former self and he relinquishes responsibility for his former self by ceasing to contemplate it.

Inauthentic people maintain particular projects of avoiding responsibility for their present situation or their past deeds by refusing, in bad faith, to acknowledge that they are responsible. More specifically, they refuse to acknowledge the inability of the self to coincide with itself as a facticity or as a pure transcendence, and they refuse to acknowledge the unlimited freedom of the self and the implications of this unlimited freedom. Recall Sartre's arguments to the effect that the for-itself, as nothing but the negation of the in-itself, is founded upon what it is not. It cannot, therefore, become its own foundation or coincide with itself as a for-itself-in-itself. There is nothing that the for-itself can be without having to be it. Unable to be what it is, the for-itself must perpetually choose what it is. It cannot not choose its responses to its situation, and because its responses to its situation are chosen, it is responsible for its choices. Even if the for-itself chooses to do nothing, that is still a choice for which it is responsible.

In Sartre's view, inauthenticity is the denial of the cardinal truth that we are free and responsible; whereas authenticity, as the antithesis of inauthenticity, is the acceptance or affirmation of this cardinal truth. Sartre argues that authenticity involves a person confronting reality and facing up to the hard truth that they are a limitlessly free being that will never obtain coincidence with itself as a for-itself-in-itself. Whereas the inauthentic person seeks to avoid recognizing that this is the fundamental truth of his being, the authentic person not only recognizes it, he strives to come to terms with it and even to treat it as a source of values. The authentic person responds fully to the appeal to 'get real' that pervades Sartre's existentialism. Sartre expresses these views of the authentic person in his *War Diaries*, an early but posthumously published work in which the issue of authenticity is raised repeatedly.[1]

In his *War Diaries* Sartre argues that authenticity 'consists in adopting human reality as one's own' (*WD*, p. 113). As a radical conversion that involves a person affirming what in truth he has always been – a free and responsible being lacking coincidence with himself – adopting human reality as his own does not involve a radical change of being. Rather, it involves a radical shift in his attitude towards himself and his ineluctable situatedness. Instead of exercising his freedom in order to deny his freedom, instead of choosing not to choose, the authentic person assumes his freedom. Assuming his freedom involves assuming full responsibility for himself in the situation in which he currently finds himself. It involves accepting that this and no other is his situation: that this situation is the facticity in terms of which he must now choose himself. If he is not imprisoned he can, of course, reject his situation by running away, but this still involves a choice. A choice, moreover, that gives rise to new situations and to new demands to choose.[2] 'We have seen that it [consciousness] renounces its possibles [*sic*] only by acquiring others' (*WD*, p. 113). Above all, assuming his freedom involves realizing that because he is nothing in the mode of being it, he is nothing but the choices he makes in his situation. To clarify these points Sartre considers an example from his own life.

In his *War Diaries* Sartre considers his inauthentic friend Paul who, at the time of writing, is a soldier. Paul is not a soldier in the mode of being one. He is not a soldier-thing. In so far as he fights in an army, however, 'soldier' is the transcendent meaning of his conduct. Paul declares, 'Me, a soldier? I consider myself a civilian in military disguise' (*WD*, p. 112). For Sartre, this declaration reveals that Paul is not taking responsibility for his choices. 'He thus stubbornly continues to *flee* what he's *making of himself*' (*WD*, p. 112). Paul flees what he is making of himself – a soldier – towards the nonexistent being-in-itself of the civilian that he mistakenly fancies himself to be. In Sartre's view, Paul is an example of a 'buffeted consciousness' (*WD*, p. 112). He has not accepted his 'being-in-situation' (*WD*, p. 54). In denying that he is only ever his response to his facticity Paul pleads the excuse of his facticity. He chooses to see himself as a facticity, as a given entity swept along by circumstances. 'We shall designate this state buffeted human reality, for it realises itself as buffeted amid the possibles [*sic*], like a plank amid the waves' (*WD*, p. 111). It is in ceasing to be like Paul and accepting his being-in-situation that a person ceases to be a buffeted consciousness and becomes authentic.

To be authentic is to realise fully one's being-in-situation, whatever this situation may happen to be, with a profound awareness that, through the authentic realisation of the being-in-situation, one brings to plenary existence the situation on the one hand and human reality on the other. This presupposes a patient study of what the situation requires, and then a way of throwing oneself into it and determining oneself to 'be-for' this situation (*WD*, p. 54).

Imagine an alternative reality in which Paul is authentic. How does an authentic Paul behave? An authentic Paul recognizes that his present situation requires him to play to the full the role of a soldier. This does not mean that he pretends to be a soldier. Pretending to be a soldier is what inauthentic Paul does by considering himself to be a civilian in military disguise. In playing at being a soldier to the full, authentic Paul aims at being a soldier to the best of his ability, determining himself to 'be-for' the military situation and absorbing himself in that situation. He does not believe he is a soldier in the mode of being one, but neither does he disbelieve he is a soldier in the sense of believing that he is really something other than a soldier, something other than his current role. The same can be said for him as was said earlier for Sartre's waiter: he absorbs himself in his performance to the extent that he does not reflect upon the fact that he is performing. He has become his performance and his attitude towards himself involves a suspension of disbelief. Sartre's waiter is often held to be in bad faith, but if his attitude is the same as the attitude of an authentic Paul then he must actually be authentic.

Authenticity is not simply a matter of a person recognizing that there are no excuses for his actions, he must resist by an act of will any desire for excuses. 'Of course, it's a question not just of *recognising* that one has no excuse, but also of *willing* it' (*WD*, p. 113). Authentic Paul not only recognizes that in his current situation there are no excuses not to play at being a soldier, he does not want there be any excuses. To be truly authentic, Paul must fully realize his being-in-situation without regret. If authentic Paul does not want to be where he is he will leave without regret and face the consequences of desertion without regret. If he stays, he will assume responsibility for his staying and throw himself into the spirit of things. Sartre, as he recounts in his *War Diaries*, attempted to do just this. Rather than complain that he was really a Parisian intellectual forced by circumstances to join an army unit in an obscure region of France, he attempted to make the most of his situation and to dedicate himself without remorse to his current role of 'soldier' – albeit a soldier with few duties who was often at liberty to read and write for sixteen hours a day.

The idea that living authentically involves living without regret is central to Nietzsche's view of authenticity. Similarities between the respective positions of Sartre and Nietzsche are explored in the next chapter.

Authenticity, as noted, involves a person coming to terms with the fact that he will never achieve the substantiality of a for-itself-in-itself. Contrary to what might be supposed, however, authenticity does not involve abandoning the desire for substantiality and foundation. The desire to be its own foundation belongs to the immediate ontological structure of the for-itself, and so the for-itself cannot abandon this desire. 'The first value and first object of will is: to be its own foundation. This mustn't be understood as an empty psychological desire, but as the transcendental structure of human reality' (*WD*, p. 110). Any attempt to abandon altogether the desire for foundation collapses into the project of nihilism considered earlier. As noted, in seeking to escape the desire for foundation a nihilist aims to be a non-being-in-itself. He is as much in bad faith as the person who aims to be a being-in-itself.

The project of authenticity is still motivated by the search for substantiality and foundation, but it differs crucially from bad faith in that 'it suppresses that which, in the search, is flight' (*WD*, p. 112). The authentic person does not aim at substantiality by means of a futile flight from his freedom. Instead, he aims at substantiality by continually founding himself upon the affirmation of his freedom. The affirmation of his freedom is assumed as his basic principle or ultimate value. He seeks to identify himself with his inalienable freedom rather than flee his inalienable freedom in the vain hope of identifying himself with the in-itself. The project of authenticity is actually more successful at achieving a kind of substantiality than the project of inauthenticity, because the project of authenticity reconciles a person to what he really is, an essentially free being, whereas the project of inauthenticity is only ever a flight from what a person really is towards an unachievable identity with the in-itself. In fleeing freedom a person does not establish a foundation, but in assuming his freedom he establishes freedom itself as a foundation. In assuming his freedom he 'becomes' what he is (free) rather than failing to become what he can never be (unfree). The desire for constancy can only be satisfied by embracing freedom because freedom is the only thing about a person that is constant. 'Thus authenticity is a value but not primary. It gives itself as a means to arrive at substantiality' (*WD*, p. 112).

It is important to stress that the form of substantiality arrived at through authenticity is not a fixed state of being. As noted, it is logically impossible for the for-itself to obtain a fixed state of being by any means, and all attempts to do so function in bad faith. The substantiality obtained through authenticity is not achieved by the for-itself once and for all; it is a substantiality that has to be continually self-perpetuated and perpetually reassumed. In keeping with Sartre's general maxim, a person cannot simply *be* authentic, he *has to be* authentic. To declare that he is authentic in the mode of a thing, as a table is a table, is to slide back into bad faith. As Ronald Santoni points out: 'The project of tying down one's authenticity can also become – as does sincerity – a project of inauthenticity' (Santoni 1995, p. 95). Authentic being is not a permanent foundation that a person can choose to establish once and for all at a particular time, but rather a metastable foundation that he must maintain by constantly choosing authentic responses to his situation. 'So it is by no means enough to be authentic: it's necessary to adapt one's life to one's authenticity' (*WD*, p. 221). Authenticity is not an essence, it is the way a person chooses to respond to his facticity and the way in which he chooses himself in response to his facticity. Authenticity is the continued task of choosing responses that affirm freedom and responsibility rather than responses that signify a flight from freedom and responsibility. The authentic person takes on the task of continually resisting the slide into bad faith that threatens every project.

I will now critically examine Sartre's view of authenticity.

If Sartrean authenticity involves living without regret, then the following objection regarding the very possibility of authenticity suggests itself: arguably, authenticity is impossible because it is impossible to live without regret. Regret, it seems, is an unavoidable part of the human condition because anyone with the capacity to imagine alternatives cannot help wishing, at least occasionally, that they had made a different choice. Sartre's reply to this objection would probably be that this does not show authenticity is impossible, simply that it is very difficult to achieve. If a person can come to regret less, as undoubtedly he can by employing various strategies from psychotherapy to the study of existentialism, then arguably he has the potential to master himself completely and regret nothing. If pressed, Sartre might concede that the task of complete self-mastery and self-overcoming is too difficult to achieve in one lifetime, particularly for people raised in a culture of regret and recrimination. Yet he would still insist that it is an heroic ideal worth striving for because it is always better to get real, get a grip and make a stand than it is to be a buffeted consciousness. It is better, not least, because a person who constantly strives to confront his situation and overcome it, a person who thereby constantly strives to confront and overcome himself, gains nobility and self-respect. A cowardly person, on the other hand, who dwells on regret, refusing to confront his situation and his being in that situation, knows only his own weakness and sense of defeat.

Arguably, authentic existence as a sustained project can be striven for and is worth striving for, but it cannot be achieved. It is the holy grail of existentialism – its unattainable ideal. Sustained authenticity is conceivable as a logical possibility, but no one can actually achieve it. It is like living without making errors of judgement. We know what it would be to live without making errors of judgement, but there will never be a person who makes no errors of judgement. As Sartre acknowledges, bad faith threatens every project of the human being. A person would have to be superhuman always to avoid sliding into bad faith. A person slides into bad faith the moment he ceases consciously resisting the world's endless temptations to slide. Bad faith is too convenient and too seductive to be avoided at all times.

Considering the world's endless temptations to slide into bad faith and the difficulties people face in resisting them, Sartre takes the example of a family man who is called to war (*WD*, pp. 220–1). Prior to his call-up the man is a typical bourgeois who treats his life as though it is on rails with a course dictated by the expectations of his family and his profession. He allows himself to be what others want him to be. The stark realities of war open his eyes and inspire him to put his life into perspective. He assumes his freedom and becomes his

own man. 'He's led to *think* about those [past] situations, to make resolutions for the future, and to establish guidelines for *keeping* authenticity as he moves on to other events' (*WD*, pp. 220–1). He has become
a warrior and wishes to remain a warrior even after the war. A man
who is ready for anything, a man who takes responsibility for himself
and does not make excuses. A strong, silent type who refuses to compromise himself or to say what others want to hear just because they
want to hear it. Resistance to his noble resolution comes not from
within him but from the world and from his own past. 'Resistance
comes, not from residues of inauthenticity which may remain here
and there in a badly dusted-off consciousness, but simply from the
fact that his previous situations resist the change as *things*' (*WD*,
p. 221). His wife, whom he still loves, comes to visit him at the front
with all the expectations he has so faithfully fulfilled in the past.
Without any effort or intention he behaves differently towards her
simply because he is different. Her expectations, however, present him
with the image of his former inauthentic self. This is the real test of
his new-found authenticity because 'he can't revert to his old errors
vis-à-vis that woman without, at a stroke, tumbling headlong into
inauthenticity' (*WD*, p. 221). His love for his wife means that it is
likely he will slide into inauthenticity by conforming to her expectations of him: 'For, presumably, a being who expects the inauthentic of
us will freeze us to the marrow with inauthenticity, by reviving our old
love' (*WD*, p. 221). Sartre goes on to say, 'It is an imposed inauthenticity, against which it is easy but painful to defend oneself' (*WD*,
p. 221). This last remark is perplexing. If imposed inauthenticity is
painful to resist then how can it be easy to resist? If it is by virtue of
his love for his wife that the man succumbs to imposed inauthenticity
then it is as difficult for him to resist imposed inauthenticity as it is for
him to resist loving his wife. Sartre would reply that it is in fact easy
for the man to stop loving his wife and so resist imposed inauthenticity because there is no inertia in consciousness and love is only the
choice to be in love. Objections to Sartre's view that there is no inertia
in consciousness were considered earlier in this book when I criticized
his radical freedom thesis and his claim that emotional states have no
momentum of their own.

As suggested, the difficulties facing a person striving for sustained
authentic existence are apparently insurmountable. In his *War Diaries*
Sartre acknowledges his own failure to achieve sustained authentic
existence. 'I am not authentic, I have halted on the threshold of the

promised lands. But at least I point the way to them and others can go there' (*WD*, p. 62). Sartre does not say, however, why others should achieve what he, of all people, fails to achieve. If the great champion of authenticity with his superior mental strength and his deep determination cannot achieve authentic existence, what hope is there for others?

To summarize: Authentic existence is a project that has to be continually reassumed. A person is only as authentic as his present act. Even if he has been consistently authentic for a week, if he is not authentic right now then he is not authentic. Given the world's endless temptations to bad faith, the difficulties of resisting regret and imposed inauthenticity, the fact that habit and other's expectations shape a person's being as much as his capacity to choose, it is unrealistic to suppose that anyone can sustain authenticity for a significant period of time. At best, it appears a person can be authentic occasionally, which does not amount to achieving authentic existence as a sustained project. Authentic existence – the sustained project – is an unobtainable existentialist ideal. Nevertheless, it is an ideal worth aiming at.

Another criticism that can be levelled against Sartre is that the pursuit of authenticity as he defines it is necessarily an intellectual project. Seemingly, the pursuit of authenticity requires a person to be intellectually aware of certain truths about the human condition. To affirm freedom as an ultimate goal, for example, it seems a person must first realize the futility of trying to achieve coincidence with himself as a for-itself-in-itself. When Sartre criticizes a person for his inauthenticity he does not seem fully to appreciate that the person may simply not realize he is inauthentic. The person may genuinely believe, knowing no better, that it is possible for him to coincide with himself. He will not, of course, present his belief to himself in such intellectual terms. His belief will take the form of a faith in the possibility of satisfying all his desires and achieving complete fulfilment. Similarly, if a person is not aware of the existential truth that he is only his being-in-situation then inevitably he will believe that he is what he has always been rather than what he has suddenly become. He will believe, for example, that he is a civilian in disguise rather than a soldier, if the role of civilian is all he knew prior to his conscription.

Against this criticism, Sartre would insist that it only takes limited intelligence to recognize the existential truths of the human condition. They are not esoteric truths buried in obscure works of philosophy. Everyday life is replete with lessons in the elusiveness of satisfaction, the imminence of death, the contingency of existence, and so on. If people do not see these existential truths, and the implications of these truths, it is not because they are uninformed, but because they refuse to confront them. It is because they are exercising wilful ignorance motivated by cowardice and sustained by bad faith. In most cases, it is not because people lack the intelligence that they do not see the existential truths of the human condition, but because they do not want to see them. That they do not want to see them implies, of course, that they have already seen them. Having already seen them and having experienced terrible anxiety at the sight of them, however, they desperately want to avoid seeing them again. The means by which they avoid seeing them again is bad faith. As argued, bad faith is a coping strategy by means of which people avoid overwhelming anguish. If this is so then ironically there is a kind of wisdom in the wilful ignorance of people who lack the courage to confront the hard truths of the human condition.[3]

If the pursuit of authenticity was necessarily an intellectual project, then only educated people would pursue authenticity, which is not the case. History shows that uneducated people strive to assume their freedom, just as it shows that an expert in the theory of existentialism can give way to the inauthenticity of anti-Semitism.[4] Although the pursuit of authenticity need not necessarily be an intellectual project, some people are, nevertheless, inspired to pursue authenticity as a direct result of studying existentialism. Studying existentialism highlights existential truths, exposes bad faith and emphasizes the necessity of freedom and responsibility. Studying existentialism can be a process of profound personal enlightenment that influences the very nature of a person's being in the world. In an age when philosophy is often regarded simply as an academic subject alongside other academic subjects, the claim that profound personal enlightenment can result from the study of philosophy sounds grandiose. According to the founders of the Western philosophical tradition, however, achieving personal enlightenment is precisely the purpose of studying philosophy. For Plato, for example, the purpose of studying philosophy, especially his philosophy, is to achieve knowledge of the fundamental truths that enable a person to distinguish appearance from reality. Like Platonism, although its worldview is very different, existentialism offers enlightenment and a way out of the cave.[5]

A final criticism that can be levelled against Sartre is that his view of authenticity appears to contain the following contradiction. On the one hand, he argues that to be authentic a person must realize his being-in-situation by throwing himself wholeheartedly into his situation. On the other hand, he argues that authenticity involves refusing to live according to the expectations of others. Recall Sartre's example of the former family-man turned soldier who is visited at the front by his wife. Sartre argues that the man cannot conform to his wife's former image of him without falling into inauthenticity. But how can a person throw himself into certain situations without conforming to the expectations of others? Conforming to the expectations of others is precisely what a committed response to certain situations requires. If the man is to throw himself wholeheartedly into his present situation – not the war but his meeting with his beloved wife – he must indulge her and make an effort to live up to her expectations of him in order to comfort her and preserve his relationship with her. It could be argued that such behaviour would be patronizing, but if patronizing someone involves treating them in a condescending manner then the man would patronize his wife far more if, having experienced horrors unknown to her, he confronted her in a manner superior, sullen and harsh. Suppose the man refuses to indulge his wife and says to her, 'This war has put me in touch with the real me and I can no longer behave the way I used to.' A reasonable response to this remark would be that if the war really has put him in touch with himself then he ought to realize that he is free to adapt his behaviour to the requirements of any situation. To drive away a wife that he still loves because he cannot allow himself to conform to a former image of himself is not the behaviour of an authentic hero, but the behaviour of an inflexible, self-destructive fool. Authenticity, it has been argued, is an heroic ideal. The archetypal hero is both a lover and a fighter and can love or fight according to the demands of the situation. Moreover, his capacity to love is not corrupted by his capacity to fight, hate and face horrors, any more than his capacity to fight is weakened by his capacity to love.

To be fair to Sartre it must be noted that as he grew older, and particularly after the Second World War, he began to acknowledge that authenticity involves conforming to some extent to the expectations of others. His later writings acknowledge that a degree of social conformity is required for a person to meet the demands of most situations because most situations are to some extent human social situations. People, he argues, are responsible for living up to the expectations that result from their social and historical circumstances. A person who seeks to evade this responsibility by refusing to be a person of his time acts in bad faith. He acts as though he is a being-in-itself rather than a being founded upon the situation of his day and age. In *Anti-Semite and Jew* Sartre even argues that it is authentic for a person raised in the Jewish culture to conform to the expectations of that culture by choosing himself as a Jew. He argues that it would be inauthentic for the same person to choose not to be a Jew because this choice of himself would be a denial of his situation and the 'Jewish reality' (*AJ*, p. 137) that constitutes his ethnic, cultural and historical facticity. Like Sartre's homosexual (*BN*, p. 63), the inauthentic Jew would have it that he is a pure transcendence, when in fact he is and must be the transcendence of his facticity.

CHAPTER 8

SARTRE AND NIETZSCHE

We, however, *want to become those we are* – human beings who are new, unique, incomparable, who give themselves laws, who create themselves.

(Nietzsche, *The Gay Science*, 335, p. 266)

Sartre and Nietzsche hold similar views on authenticity. Comparing their views sheds further light on the phenomenon of authenticity.

Bad faith is a choice not to choose. As such it can be described as negative freedom that exercises itself in denying, checking and repressing itself. Freedom is often exercised in this way in accordance with what Nietzsche refers to in *The Genealogy of Morals* as the ascetic ideal. To adopt the ascetic ideal is to value self-repression and self-denial for their own sake and above all else. A person who adopts the ascetic ideal does not, for example, value chastity for the sexual health and peace of mind it can bring, but solely for the self-denial it involves. Opposed to the ascetic ideal is Nietzsche's notion of the noble ideal. The noble ideal involves the positive affirmation of freedom. A noble person positively affirms himself as a free being. He does not concern himself with denying and repressing his freedom but enjoys it and is constantly aware of it. He does this through decisive action, through overcoming and self-overcoming, through the acceptance of self-responsibility and the refusal to regret and, above all, through the choice of his own values. For Nietzsche, positive freedom is expansive, sometimes even recklessly or violently so. It glories in its own strength as a positive will to power.

Will to power, a key notion in Nietzsche's thought, can be either positive or negative. Positive will to power is power as it is most commonly understood: power that is expansive or even explosive.

According to Nietzsche, however, the opposite is also will to power. A being that refuses to expand still has will to power. Its will is not a will to exist rather than a will to power. 'For what does not exist cannot will, but that which is in existence, how could it still want to come into existence? Only where life is, there is also will: not will to life, but – so I teach you – will to power' (Nietzsche 1988, p. 138). An army making a tactical retreat refuses expansion, but it has not thereby lost its will to power. Similarly, a person who conserves his strength behind raised defences exercises will to power in inviting his enemy to expend his strength against those defences. According to Nietzsche, a person cannot *not* be a will to power, just as, according to Sartre, a person cannot *not* be free. Whereas Nietzsche has the concepts of positive and negative will to power, or strong and weak will to power, Sartre has the concepts of the positive freedom of the responsible, authentic person and the negative freedom of the inauthentic person who acts in bad faith choosing not to choose.[1]

Sartre argues that freedom can value itself as the source of all values. This positive freedom projects itself in accordance with the principles of Nietzsche's noble ideal. It is a positive will to power. A person does not achieve a radical conversion to authenticity by rejecting and divorcing his former self through the exercise of sincerity or insincerity, but by overcoming his former self, his former values, to become the creator of his own values. There is a definite sense in which, for Sartre, radical conversion to authenticity involves a person becoming something akin to Nietzsche's *Übermensch*. '*Übermensch*' literally means 'overman'; the man who has overcome himself. As the creator of his own values the overman creates himself; he is the artist or author of his own life.[2]

Whatever a negative person or a person in bad faith identifies as a bad experience to be forgotten or denied, the artist or author of his own life, whose aim is positively to affirm his entire life, will identify as a learning experience that helped to make him stronger and wiser. He regrets nothing because every experience has contributed to making him what he is. In Nietzsche's view, he will not even regret his evil qualities, or what other people may label his evil qualities. As the source of his own values he will re-evaluate his evil qualities as his best qualities. His ability to do this is a true mark of his authenticity. 'The great epochs of our life are the occasions when we gain the courage to rebaptize our evil qualities as our best qualities' (Nietzsche 1990a, 116, p. 97).

It is time to return to the examination set aside earlier of Dostoevsky's character Raskolnikov. Although Raskolnikov tells himself he must strive to be like Napoleon, a man who has the strength of character to justify his crimes to himself, unlike Napoleon, Raskolnikov lacks the courage 'to redeem the past and to transform every "it was" into "thus I willed it"' (Nietzsche 1988, p. 161).

As Raskolnikov's ego is not sufficient to swallow the enormity of his crime, his only means of escaping his guilt is to lapse into an attitude of bad faith whereby he disowns himself by disowning his past.

To disown the past in bad faith and to redefine the past by assuming responsibility for it are radically different responses. If the aspiring convert to authenticity is to overcome bad faith he must take responsibility for the whole of his past without regret. A person who regrets wishes his past were different; he wishes he were not the free being he is and has been. A person who regrets fails to affirm the whole of his freedom and hence the whole of his life as the creation of his freedom. Nietzsche holds that the highest affirmation of life is the desire for eternal recurrence. For a person to truly affirm his freedom and his life as the creation of his freedom he must embrace the possibility of living it all over again in every detail an infinite number of times. Nietzsche's answer to the perennial moral question 'How should I live?' is this: aspire to live in such a way that you want each and every moment of your life to recur eternally. Nietzsche, in *Ecce Homo*, calls this his formula for greatness: 'My formula for greatness for a human being is *amor fati*: that one wants nothing to be other than it is, not in the future, not in the past, not in all eternity' (Nietzsche 1979, p. 68).

In rejecting and discarding his past like an old skin, Raskolnikov fails to adopt Nietzsche's formula for greatness. In Nietzsche's words, which may be an allusion to Dostoevsky's Raskolnikov: 'An image made this pale man pale. He was equal to his deed when he did it: but he could not endure its image after it was done' (Nietzsche 1988, p. 65).

Apparently conflicting claims have been made in this book regarding the nature of the person who has overcome bad faith. It was at least suggested that he would be a deranged, anguish-ridden psychotic like Roquentin, the main character of Sartre's novel *Nausea*. Now it is being argued that he would be a noble, life-affirming overman. What is to be made of this?

All faith is bad faith in the sense that all faith involves a state of false consciousness in which a person does not believe that his belief is a belief. Not all faith is bad, however, in the sense that it is best overcome. There is a need to distinguish between particular projects of bad faith that may be negative or even morally bad, and the primitive project of bad faith that is vital for personal development and psychological well-being. Although the overman has overcome bad faith with regard to regrets, excuses and apologies, he has not overcome and does not want to overcome his faith in himself, his faith in his own performance. Like Sartre's waiter who plays with his being in order to realize it, the overman makes-believe he is such and such, without thereby believing or disbelieving that he is such and such. The insane person like Roquentin, on the other hand, has lost faith in himself as a performance. In recognizing all faith for what it is – a state of false consciousness – and realizing that there is nothing that he is or can be in the mode of being it, he attempts to be true to himself. As a result, he finds himself unable to make-believe he is anything at all. In finding himself unable to make-believe he is anything at all, he comes to believe he is nothing at all: a non-being-in-itself. In believing this, however, he does not overcome bad faith. As argued, it is bad faith for a person to believe that he is his own nothingness in the mode of being it. The attempt to overcome all bad faith, including the primitive project of bad faith, results in a fall into the most desperate particular project of bad faith: the faith of nihilism.

Similar ideas to those expressed above are put forward by Joseph Catalano who distinguishes between weak and strong notions of good and bad faith. He writes: 'one can live in bad faith, in the weak sense, while also living in good faith in the strong sense' (Catalano 1993, p. 88). Catalano's notion of weak bad faith applies, for example, to the bad faith of a waiter who plays at being a waiter without thereby aiming to become a waiter in the mode of being one, while his notion of strong bad faith applies to the bad faith of a waiter who plays at being a waiter with the aim of becoming a waiter in the mode of being one. Catalano's notion of weak good faith applies to a person's vague realization that bad faith is inescapable given his need to play some role or other and to adopt a fixed viewpoint upon himself: 'in the weak sense, our good faith is only a fleeting realization that we cannot escape bad faith itself' (Catalano 1993, p. 81). Finally, his notion of strong good faith applies to the positive affirmation of freedom.[3] The overman, in not believing that he is such and such, avoids bad faith in Catalano's strong sense, but in maintaining his faith in his own performance he lives in bad faith in Catalano's weak sense. Also, as an authentic person who assumes his freedom and takes responsibility for himself without regret, he lives in good faith in Catalano's strong sense. To be an overman he must live in this way, otherwise his ability to live in strong good faith as an authentic person would be undermined by a lack of weak bad faith amounting to a nihilistic lack of faith in his own performance.

CHAPTER 9

SARTRE AND HEIDEGGER

> Anticipation, however, unlike inauthentic being-towards-death, does not evade the fact that death is not to be outstripped; instead, anticipation frees itself *for* accepting this.
>
> (Heidegger, *Being and Time*, p. 308)

Sartre and Heidegger hold similar views on authenticity. Comparing their views sheds further light on the phenomenon of authenticity.

Like Sartre, Heidegger holds that the project of authenticity involves a person affirming the inescapable truths of the human condition. Sartre's account of authenticity emphasizes the assumption and affirmation of freedom, whereas Heidegger's account emphasizes the assumption and affirmation of mortality. Authenticity for Heidegger is primarily authentic being-towards-death (Heidegger 1993, p. 304). Although Sartre agrees with much of what Heidegger says about authenticity, he has some doubts about his notion of being-towards-death. I will consider these doubts when I have outlined Heidegger's position.

Dasein, the phenomenon at the heart of Heidegger's philosophy, was considered earlier in this book. *Dasein* refers to a person's unique spatial and temporal situatedness in the world. Heidegger argues that 'Death is Dasein's *ownmost* possibility (Heidegger 1993, p. 307).[1] The constant possibility of death in the present, the inevitability of death in the future, is internal to the very being of *Dasein*. A person's present is what it is by virtue of its finitude, a finitude arising from the promise of death that perpetually haunts the present. Authentic being-towards-death involves a person fully acknowledging finitude and the inevitability of death in the way he lives his life. By recognizing that he himself must die, rather than merely recognizing that people die, a person ceases to view himself in bad faith as simply another other and realizes that he exists as the wholly unique possibility of his own death: 'The non-relational character of death, as understood in anticipation, individualises Dasein down to itself' (Heidegger 1993, p. 308). Only by realizing that he is the wholly unique possibility of his own death does he cease to treat himself as though he is a copy of the next man and of all men. For Heidegger, this is the real meaning of authenticity. The authentic person, like the authentic artefact, is the genuine, bona fide article, not a reproduction or a replica. Though his life may resemble the lives of many others, he is nonetheless his own person and he identifies himself as such. The following passage from David Cooper's *Heidegger* provides an excellent summary of the above:

> Once I do range the possibilities ahead of me in anticipation of their coming to an end, I also come to recognize the unique individuality of my life. For while the episodes which belong to it – getting married, becoming a lecturer, and so on – are ones that might figure in anyone else's life, the way in which I gather them into an integrated whole is uniquely mine. This is what Heidegger means when he writes that my death cannot be delegated, that 'no one can take the Other's dying away from him' [*Being and Time*, p. 284]. The point is not that a person cannot die in another's place: think of Sidney Carton taking Charles Darnay's place on the scaffold [Charles Dickens, *A Tale of Two Cities*]. It is, rather, that dying in the sense of living in anticipation of death is necessarily an individual path. (Cooper 1996, p. 42)

In Heidegger's view, it is only when a person fully realizes that he must die, and acts in accordance with this realization, that he truly begins to exist and live in his own right. In taking responsibility for his own death he takes responsibility for his own life and the way in which he chooses to live it. For Heidegger, to truly realize and affirm mortality is to overcome bad faith. This view, despite Sartre's yet-to-be-considered reservations regarding being-towards-death, concurs with his claim that authenticity involves living without regret. If the positive affirmation of freedom demands that a person affirm his entire life without regret, then it follows that he must also affirm his mortality. This affirmation would not involve relishing the prospect of death – it is not a suicidal tendency – but it would involve a person acknowledging that his life is finite and the implications that this has for the way he lives his life.

A key characteristic of Nietzsche's overman, who was compared earlier with Sartre's radical convert to authenticity, is his recognition and acceptance of his own mortality. The overman is a person who, though fully aware of his mortality, is not petrified with fear at the thought of it. He does not allow his fear of death to prevent him from taking certain risks and living his life to the full. Simone de Beauvoir argues that this attitude towards death is an essential characteristic of the adventurous person who values the affirmation of his freedom above timid self-preservation. 'Even his death is not an evil since he is a man only in so far as he is mortal: he must assume it as the natural limit of his life, as the risk implied by every step' (de Beauvoir 2000, p. 82). Unadventurous people who fail to live life to the full because they fear death still die. They die, however, never having really lived; having already died, metaphorically, many times.

> Cowards die many times before their deaths;
> The valiant never taste of death but once.
> (Shakespeare, *Julius Caesar*, II, ii).

Although Heidegger's thoughts on affirming mortality concur with Sartre's thoughts on affirming freedom, the fact remains that Sartre objects to the concept of being-towards-death that lies at the heart of Heidegger's theory of authenticity. What is to be made of this?

Common ground exists between Heidegger and Sartre because Sartre agrees with Heidegger that embracing life's finitude is a prompt to authentic action. He agrees with Heidegger that a person who embraces his finitude is motivated to plunge into situations bravely rather than hold back in timid and ultimately futile self-preservation. He agrees also that embracing finitude inspires a person to reject mediocrity (what Heidegger calls everydayness) in favour of being all that he can be. Sartre, however, disagrees with Heidegger that death is a person's *ownmost* possibility. Indeed, Sartre argues that death is not among a person's possibilities at all. As the absolute limit of all of a person's possibilities it is not itself a possibility. Against Heidegger, Sartre argues that a person does not die his own death because his own death is not an event he can experience. From his own point of view, he does not undergo death. How could he, when death is the utter annihilation of the point of view that he is? In a very real sense, death only happens to other people. Only the death of other people can be an event in my life, just as my death can only be an event in the lives of those who outlive me. In the words of Wittgenstein: 'Death is not an event in life: we do not live to experience death' (Wittgenstein 2001, prop. 6.4311).

It is, of course, claimed by some that we do experience death because death is not annihilation but a moment of transition. It is not possible to explore here the huge metaphysical assumptions involved in this claim: suffice to say that existential phenomenology rejects them as incompatible with its worldview. Certainly, if death is a moment of transition rather than annihilation then it is not death. Death, by definition, is the limit of life. If we enter an afterlife when we die then we do not really die.

In Sartre's view, a person who is genuinely aware of his mortality and lives his life accordingly is not thereby subject to a sense of being-towards-death like a condemned prisoner awaiting execution. Sartre even argues that a person who views his death as being nearer than yesterday is mistaken. He will, of course, live for a certain number of days, but he is mistaken if he thinks that with each day that passes he is using up a sort of quota. He is mistaken because he does not have a quota. He could die now, or tomorrow, or years from now. It is inevitable that he will die eventually, but the time of his death is not predetermined. When he is dead others will give the total of his years, but this total was not fixed in advance while he was alive and his life was not a process of fulfilling it. Only a condemned person has a quota of days, but as Sartre points out, even a condemned person can be reprieved unexpectedly or killed by flu before reaching the scaffold. Sartre's point is that the closeness of death changes with circumstances. If a person was in a high fever yesterday, he was closer to death yesterday than he is today now that he has recovered.

> . . . I can not say that the minute which is passing is bringing death closer to me. It is true that death is coming to me if I consider very broadly that my life is limited. But within these very elastic limits (I can die at the age of a hundred or at thirty-seven, tomorrow) I cannot know whether this end is coming closer to me or being removed further from me. This is because there is a considerable difference in *quality* between death at the limit of old age and sudden death which annihilates us at the prime of life or in our

youth. To wait for the former is to accept that life is a *limited* enterprise; it is one way among others of choosing finitude and electing our ends on the foundation of finitude. To wait for the second would be to wait with the idea that my life is an enterprise which is *lacking*. (*BN*, p. 536)

So, according to Sartre, a person does not experience his finitude as such. He does not experience himself as a being progressing towards an encounter with the nothingness and annihilation of death; as a being-towards-death.

death haunts me at the very heart of each of my projects as their inevitable reverse side. But precisely because this 'reverse' is to be assumed not as my possibility but as the possibility that there are for me no longer any possibilities, it does not penetrate me . . . this is not because death does not limit my freedom but because freedom never encounters this limit. I am not 'free to die' [as Heidegger claims], but I am a free mortal. (*BN*, pp. 547–8)

The for-itself is the expectation of nothingness, but the nothingness that the for-itself expects is not the nothingness of death but the negations or negativities that arise everywhere in its world. The for-itself can reflect, sometimes with indifference and sometimes with profound horror, that death is somewhere up ahead, but unlike Faustus awaiting the devil, it cannot feel death coming.[2]

NOTES

CHAPTER 1:   BEING-FOR-ITSELF

1 Hegel writes: 'Being, the indeterminate immediate, is in fact *nothing*, and neither more nor less than *nothing*.' He also writes: 'Nothing is . . . altogether the same as pure *being*.' And also: '*Pure being* and *pure nothing* are . . . the same' (Hegel 1998, p. 82).
2 Hegel writes:

> What is the truth is neither being nor nothing, but that being does not pass over, but has passed over, into nothing, and nothing into being . . . The truth is, therefore, this movement of the immediate vanishing of the one in the other: *becoming*, a movement in which both are distinguished, but by a difference which has equally immediately resolved itself. (Hegel 1998, pp. 82–3)

3 Sartre's use of the term 'the understanding' here need not be confusing if it is understood that non-being is the logical ground for the possibility of the understanding. Indeed, the term 'the understanding' could arguably be replaced by the term 'non-being' here without doing violence to its meaning.
4 R.D. Laing writes: 'There is a common illusion that one somehow increases one's understanding of a person if one can translate a personal understanding of him into the impersonal terms of a sequence or system of *it*-processes' (Laing 1990, p. 22).
5 Mary Midgley writes:

> The really monstrous thing about existentialism too is its proceeding as if the world contained only dead matter (things) on the one hand and fully rational, educated, adult human beings on the other – as if there were no other life-forms. The impression of *desertion* or *abandonment* which existentialists have is due, I am sure, not to the removal of God, but to this contemptuous dismissal of almost the whole biosphere – plants, animals, and children. Life shrinks to a few urban rooms; no wonder it becomes absurd. (Midgley 2002, pp. 18–19)

6 Hegel writes: 'The living substance is that being which is truly subject . . . As subject it is pure and simple negativity' (Hegel 2003, p. 16).

7 In his *Meditations* Descartes attempts to prove the existence of the external world. He does this by arguing that God, by virtue of his moral perfection and inability to deceive, guarantees the existence of an external world corresponding to the ideas people have of it. Descartes' claim to the existence of God rests upon a version of the Ontological Argument first put forward by Anselm in his *Proslogion*. According to Anselm, it is a contradiction to reject the predicate 'exists' while retaining the subject 'God'. In other words, the most perfect conceivable entity must exist, otherwise it would lack that attribute and therefore not be perfect. Descartes, then, believes he has only to appeal to his idea of God in order to prove the existence of that which in turn guarantees the existence of the external world. Kant refutes the Ontological Argument by arguing that even if it is a contradiction to reject the predicate 'exists' while retaining the subject 'God', there is no contradiction involved in rejecting both subject and predicate. As he writes in his *Critique of Pure Reason*: 'the unconditioned necessity of a judgement is not the same as the absolute necessity of things . . , If we say, "There is no God" neither the omnipotence nor any other of its predicates is given, they are one and all rejected together with the subject' (Kant 1990, pp. 501–2). In so far as Kant's refutation undermines the Ontological Argument upon which Descartes' proof of God's existence rests, Descartes cannot resort to God as a means of overcoming his solipsistic difficulties.

8 Berkeley's idealism is well summed up in the following passage from his *Principles of Human Knowledge*:

> All those bodies which compose the mighty frame of the world, have not any subsistence without a mind, that their being is to be perceived or known; that consequently so long as they are not actually perceived by me, or do not exist in my mind or that of any other created spirit, they must either have no existence at all, or else subsist in the mind of some eternal spirit'. (Berkeley 1988, p. 55)

9 In his *Monadology* Leibniz, thinking along similar lines, writes:

> Suppose that there were a machine so constructed as to produce thought, feeling and perception, we could imagine it increased in size while retaining the same proportions, so that one could enter as one might a mill. On going inside we should only see the parts impinging upon one another, we should not see anything which would explain a perception. (Leibniz 1990a, p. 181)

10 Henry Allison emphasizes this 'two standpoint' interpretation of Kant, when he writes:

> The object to which I refer my representations must be described merely as a transcendental object, not as a noumenon, because I am lacking a faculty of nonsensible intuition. The underlying assump-

tion is that if I had such a faculty, the object would be a genuine noumenon, and I would know it as it is in itself. (Allison 1983, p. 245)

11 Heidegger writes: 'The nothing itself nihilates. (The nothing nothings)' (Heidegger 1978, p. 105).

12 The Gestalt theorists are among those who note that the appearance of an entity is always the appearance of a figure on a ground. The Gestalt school of psychology emerged in opposition to the psychological atomism of the empiricist tradition. Against the empiricist view that there are no innate ideas, the Gestalt theorists argue that there is a predisposition to organize the perceptual field in certain ways. Organization in terms of a figure-ground distinction is only one example. There is also a predisposition to organize basic elements of experience according to certain patterns. For example, – – –   – – – is not perceived as six separate dashes but as two groups of three.

13 In contrast to the views of Parmenides, who argues that all is One, the Pythagoreans argue that existence is comprised of spatially extended units. The pupil of Parmenides, Zeno of Elea, refutes this Pythagorean claim with a number of paradoxes, several of which aim to show that the Pythagorean conception renders motion impossible. The stadium paradox shows that if existence is comprised of discrete units then it is impossible to complete the course. Before completing the full distance a runner would have to complete half the distance, and before completing half the distance he would have to complete a quarter of the distance, and so on *ad infinitum*. Making the same point as the stadium paradox, the paradox of Achilles and the tortoise shows that within the Pythagorean conception it is impossible for Achilles to catch up with the tortoise if the tortoise is given a head start. Finally, the paradox of the arrow shows that if at any moment an arrow in flight occupies a space equal to its own dimensions then it is in fact at rest. The Pythagorean view results in the contradiction that motion is comprised of moments of rest.

14 The notion of the self as an unfulfillable lack is not the exclusive property of the existentialists, and can be traced back at least as far as the Ancient Greeks. In Plato's *Gorgias*, for example, Socrates refers to the Pythagorean conception of the soul as a leaky pitcher. 'That part of their soul which contains the appetites . . . he [Pythagoras] represents as a pitcher with holes in it, because it cannot be filled up' (Plato 1960, p. 92). The image of the leaky pitcher recalls the punishment in Hades of the daughters of Danaus who were doomed to pour water for ever into leaky vessels.

15 At the heart of Plato's metaphysics is his Theory of Forms. Plato argues that the physical world encountered through the senses is merely an appearance. True reality is the realm of universal metaphysical forms. Forms are pure essences, perfect and unchanging ideas that give particular things, events and qualities in the physical world their meaning, identity and reality. For example, particular circles in the world participate in the perfect, universal form of circularity. The universal form of

circularity provides a standard that allows particular circles in the world to be recognized as approximations to that standard. In Plato's view the physical world encountered through the senses is a kind of shadow cast by the ultimate reality of the forms.

16 Heidegger's italics.

17 'Ekstatic' is derived from the Greek *'ekstasis'* meaning 'standing out from'.

18 Joseph Fell writes:

> Sartre returns us to the negating consciousness that Heidegger is criticized for bypassing. In so doing Sartre always returns us to the non-temporal being of which that consciousness is the negation and the affirmation, the affirmation-by-negation. 'Being and *Time'* becomes 'Being and *Nothingness'* because for Sartre being is ontologically prior to time and time first arises out of the 'nothingness' of consciousness as the negation of being. (Fell 1983, p. 87)

19 When referring to non-thetic consciousness (of) consciousness the 'of' is placed in brackets to indicate that non-thetic consciousness is not, as an unqualified 'of' might suggest, a further act of consciousness. As thetic consciousness of consciousness is a further act of consciousness the 'of' is used without qualification.

20 The following passage helps to make clear what Sartre means by *transcendent psychic objects*:

> When we have experienced hatred several times toward different persons, or tenacious resentments, or protracted angers, we unify these diverse manifestations by intending a psychic disposition for producing them. This psychic disposition (I am very spiteful, I am capable of hating violently, I am ill-tempered) is naturally more and other than a mere contrivance. It is a transcendent object. (*TE*, p. 70)

CHAPTER 2: BEING-FOR-OTHERS

1 There are some forms of shame that in a certain sense a person can realize for himself, shame before God or ancestors, for example. Such forms, however, are derivatives of the primary structure. Sartre describes shame before God as 'the religious practice of shame' (*BN*, p. 221).

2 Sartre argues (*BN*, Pt 3, Ch. 3) that the basis of the masochist's pleasure is that he or she is a sex object for the Other. Being-for-others is an integral aspect of sexual relationships and sexual arousal.

3 There are, however, some relationships where a recovery of subjectivity appears to be impossible. In the relationship between a person and a CCTV camera, for example, a stable situation exists in which there is no possibility of returning the look. The transcendence of a person's transcendence by a camera cannot be reversed; a person cannot become Other for the Other and so regain his transcendence. It is not possible to outstare a camera.

4 Expressing the same thought as Sartre, Wittgenstein in his *Philosophical Investigations*, writes: 'My attitude towards him is an attitude towards a soul. I am not of the *opinion* that he has a soul' (Wittgenstein 1988, IV, p. 178).

CHAPTER 3:   THE BODY

1 Anthony Manser writes: 'Whilst I am typing this I am not conscious of my fingers, but only of what I want to say. My fingers are not even the instruments I use to write with . . . When the body is working efficiently it is not noticed' (Manser 1981, p. 13).

CHAPTER 4:   EXISTENTIAL FREEDOM

1 It became Sartre's own view that *Existentialism and Humanism* is unrepresentative. Mary Warnock writes in her introduction to *Being and Nothingness*, 'I mention this essay here only to dismiss it, as Sartre himself has dismissed it. He not only regretted its publication, but also actually denied some of its doctrines in later works' (*BN*, Intro., p. xiv). Anthony Manser writes that the reason why 'the arguments in the lecture are comparatively superficial and often inconsistent with the views put forward in *Being and Nothingness*' is that it was written for the purposes of a 'fashionable literary event' rather than a serious philosophic lecture' (Manser 1981, pp. 137, 138). Sartre, who was at the height of his popularity, was influenced by the character of his audience. His desire to both entertain and shock them resulted in the distortion of his views. Norman Greene writes, 'An indication of the level of understanding to which Sartre was addressing himself is the reported fact that the opening reference to existentialism as a humanism provoked fainting among the audience' (Greene 1980, p. 13).

2 *Fundamental choice* is a term that has a specific meaning in Sartre's philosophy. To understand the meaning of fundamental choice it is necessary to recall Sartre's claim that the for-itself is constituted as a lack of being with the fundamental project of overcoming this lack. As a lack of being the for-itself aims to be being. It aims to be a for-itself-in-itself; a being in which existence and essence are one. It aims to be God. This is the fundamental project of human reality. 'Man fundamentally is the desire to be God' (*BN*, p. 566). In the concrete situation of an individual person this general project is expressed in the form of a desire to be united with a particular mode of being that is perceived to be presently lacking. The project of seeking unity with the particular mode of being that a person perceives to be presently lacking is his particular fundamental project. His particular fundamental project is established via an original or fundamental choice whereby he chooses himself as a particular kind of lack. In choosing himself as a particular kind of lack he constantly chooses to project himself towards those ends that would overcome this lack. Indeed, his personality is comprised of the host of behaviours and attitudes that

he employs in his constant effort to overcome the particular lack that he has chosen to be.

A fundamental choice is not the product of antecedent tendencies. Rather, it is the basis of all consequent ones. As an aspect of the dawning of self-consciousness, it is an original choice of self made in response to an event in early life. The event demands that some original choice or other of self be made. Though the event may be trivial in itself, it is, nonetheless, 'the crucial event of infancy' (*BN*, p. 569). It is crucial because it is here that a person first begins to choose those responses that affirm or deny his view of himself as a certain kind of character.

As a choice of self that establishes grounds for subsequent choosing, the fundamental choice is itself groundless. Though the fundamental choice is groundless, it is nonetheless necessary in that it cannot not be made. The for-itself, as a lack of being, must choose some particular project or other through which it can aim to overcome the lack of being that it is. The fundamental project upon which the for-itself embarks depends upon the fundamental choice it makes as to the value and meaning of its own lack of being. The fundamental choice is the original and most fundamental attempt on the part of the for-itself to escape the utter contingency and superfluity of its being. By choosing itself as a particular kind of lack it hopes to make sense of its being by overcoming that lack; as though in a final act of complete overcoming it could establish an ultimate *raison d'être* for its otherwise contingent being. But of course, there can be no final act of overcoming by which the for-itself establishes itself as a determinate being. Though the for-itself constantly aims to overcome the lack that it is, it cannot do so without annihilating itself. 'Man is a useless passion' (*BN*, p. 615).

The particular fundamental choice that engenders and sustains a particular fundamental project is as unique as the person himself. 'There is naturally an infinity of possible projects as there is an infinity of possible human beings' (*BN*, p. 564). Sartre's existential psychoanalysis aims to account for a person's unique attitude and behaviour by discovering his irreducible fundamental choice of himself through an exploration of his conduct and personal history. Sartre sees this method as the correct way to proceed as opposed to the methods of traditional psychoanalysis. Although he praises some of the insights of traditional psychoanalysis he is critical of its attempts to explain people in terms of such 'pseudo-irreducibles' (*BN*, p. 568) as drives and desires. For instance, he criticizes the psychologist Paul Bourget for attempting to account for Flaubert's need to write in terms of the need to feel intensely: that is, in terms of a universal pattern which is itself in need of explanation (*BN*, p. 558). Sartre argues, as does R.D. Laing in *The Divided Self*, that to explain a person in terms of pseudo-irreducible drives and desires is to reduce him to those drives and desires, and hence to explain him away. If a person is not to be explained away he must be apprehended as a unified whole. Apprehending a person as a unified whole is achieved through a discovery of his fundamental project and the fundamental choice that engenders and sustains that project.

3 'Determination', 'determined', 'determinism'. It is ironic that determinism has emerged as a label for a school of thought that denies the possibility of free will. In the everyday world of human action, to describe a person as 'determined' is not to say he is part of a machine process that simply reacts to external causes. It is to say he has the self-determination to accomplish what might not be accomplished. 'Determination' in this context refers to the exercise of will power for the purpose of determining, as far as possible, a future utterly indeterminate in itself.

4 The notion of compulsion, as applied in law, for example, still makes sense despite this claim. It seems that the notion of compulsion must be understood in the following way: to say that a person was compelled is to say that he chose to do what any rational person would do in the face of a severe threat!

5 Simone de Beauvoir argues that the Sartre Merleau-Ponty takes to task in his *Phenomenology of Perception* is a Sartre of his own invention: a pseudo-Sartre. In an article, 'Merleau-Ponty et le pseudo-Sartrisme', she accuses Merleau-Ponty of overlooking certain key passages in *Being and Nothingness* and of decontextualizing others (de Beauvoir 1955). The result is a misrepresentation of Sartre's philosophy that, in the words of Monika Langer, 'falsifies Sartre's ontology and makes a travesty of his political thought' (Langer 1981, p. 307). Merleau-Ponty, according to de Beauvoir, fails to give full credit to Sartre's notion of facticity, confounds his notions of consciousness and subjectivity and largely ignores his references to the importance of the past. The focus of *Being and Nothingness* is not the sociohistoric world, as Langer acknowledges, but neither is its importance denied by Sartre as Merleau-Ponty suggests.

6 *Persistent vegetative state*: A medical term describing the condition of a human being expected to continue to lack any detectable higher brain function, whose biological life must be supported by medical technology. A human being in such a state is generally held to be mentally dead.

7 The possibility of hypnosis implies a great deal about the nature of the human psyche. Any theory of human behaviour and motivation that does not pay attention to the phenomenon of hypnosis, including self-hypnosis, remains inadequate. Undoubtedly, a valuable line of enquiry would be to explore in detail the implications of hypnosis for Sartre's theory of freedom.

8 As McGill points out, the uncompromising nature of Sartre's theory of freedom is to some extent a result of the historical period in which it was produced. Sartre, his thoughts increasingly influenced by political considerations, wished to counter the rising tide of fascism that culminated in the Second World War by arguing in favour of individual freedom and inalienable personal responsibility (McGill 1949, p. 340).

CHAPTER 5: THE PHENOMENON OF BAD FAITH

1 Different consciousnesses are externally related to one another. They are fundamentally separate and independent of one another; external to one

another. All communication between them requires an objective medium – the body, the world. On the other hand, each individual consciousness is internally related to its own body and to the world. It is also internally related to itself, which is to say, there are no divisions within a single consciousness comparable to the divisions holding between different consciousnesses.

2 Sartre's distinction between the reflective and the pre-reflective reflected on is a quasi-duality that should not be confused with, for example, the Freudian duality of conscious and unconscious. Sartre's notion is a quasi-duality because reflective and pre-reflective consciousness are not two distinct psychic realms, but rather, respectively, consciousness reflecting upon itself as an immediate relation to the world and consciousness as it is in its immediate relation to the world. What is most important to note in attempting to dismiss claims that this distinction amounts to a duality is that reflective consciousness does not represent a separate realm of consciousness. It is rather entirely dependent upon the pre-reflective consciousness of the world upon which it reflects. Just as the relationship between pre-reflective consciousness and the world is internal, so also is the relationship between pre-reflective and reflective consciousness.

3 It is important to note that Sartre's insistence that a person cannot be both aware and not aware of something at the same time – that he is unavoidably conscious of what is (in) his consciousness – is not an outright rejection of what is described as preconscious, unconscious or subconscious. His aim is simply to attack the strong Freudian view that thoughts can be deliberately pushed into unconsciousness by consciousness. Sartre accepts that there are many aspects of mental life that are not conscious and that much mental processing, language acquisition for example, does not and cannot occur at the level of reflection. Indeed, it would be absurd for him to suggest that our entire mental life is transparent, existing at the level of reflection. To suggest this would be to suggest, for example, that a person's entire memory – whatever he has the capacity to remember – is presently held at the level of reflective consciousness. Sartre, of course, suggests nothing of the sort. It is important, he insists, 'to distinguish between consciousness and knowledge' (*BN*, p. 570). Also, he seeks to demonstrate that the greater part of our mental life is pre-reflective; that it consists largely in an immediate, non-reflective relationship with the world. A relationship that, although clearly a conscious one, is not so much reflected on as lived.

4 In physics, 'metastable' refers to an apparent state of equilibrium maintained by that which is not inherently stable: that is, a precarious equilibrium that is not fixed but must be continually self-perpetuated.

5 Comparisons can be drawn between Sartre's view of bad faith and Nietzsche's view of the slave ethic. In *The Genealogy of Morals*, Nietzsche argues that a person who has submitted to his slavery denies the meaning of the world for himself by considering it a world that is meaningful only from the point of view of his master. The slave considers himself to be just an object in his master's world. He assumes

a position that is essentially passive, refusing to defy the master in a positive, active way. If he defies the master he defies him only internally with resentful thoughts and feelings that he avoids venting with deeds. He 'escapes' his master's will only through the flight of his own nothingness away from the realities of his situation towards nothing. Ultimately, the slave comes to view his repressed, brooding, cowardly attitude as admirable and ethical. According to Nietzsche, the slave ethic is at the heart of Christian morality.

6 Sartre also takes up the issue of playing at being what we are in his play *Crime Passionnel*. Hugo has been asked by the Proletarian Party to assassinate Hoederer. Hugo's motives are questionable. Does he want to kill Hoederer for purely political reasons, or does he want to prove to himself and to others that he is tough, daring, serious-minded and independent of his father? How Hugo is to be defined depends upon his motives. Is he a selfless assassin dedicated to a political cause, or is he a common murderer who pretends to himself that he is an assassin in order to avoid confronting his selfish motives? 'Am I playing? Am I serious? Mystery . . .' (*CP*, p. 33). Hugo becomes increasingly concerned with these questions as the play progresses.

7 In his novel *The Age of Reason*, Sartre, undoubtedly recalling his example of the waiter, describes a barman whose behaviour is like that of the waiter:

'A little while ago he had been smoking a cigarette, as vague and poetic as a flowering creeper: now he had awakened, he was rather *too much* the barman, manipulating his shaker, opening it, and tipping yellow froth into glasses with slightly superfluous precision: he was impersonating a barman. Mathieu thought . . . 'Perhaps it's inevitable, perhaps one has to choose between being nothing at all, or impersonating what one is'. (*AR*, p. 173)

8 Anthony Manser writes: 'Nowhere [in *Being and Nothingness*] is it ever suggested that the waiter is in bad faith, though I must admit to having assumed, like most other writers, that he was' (Manser 1987, p. 13).

9 Gilbert Ryle writes:

His [category] mistake lay in his innocent assumption that it was correct to speak of Christ Church, The Bodleian Library, The Ashmolean Museum *and* the University, to speak, that is, as if 'the University' stood for an extra member of the class of which these other units are members. He was mistakenly allocating the University to the same category as that to which the other institutions belong. (Ryle 1990, p. 18)

10 Sartre's treatment of 'pederast' and 'homosexual' as synonymous terms is an unfortunate error offensive to homosexuals. While the particular character Sartre has in mind in his example may well have been a pederast, he fails to acknowledge that although a pederast is a homosexual the vast majority of homosexuals are not pederasts. Sartre's confusion of terms is not 'politically incorrect'; it is incorrect.

11 Lucien Fleurier, the main character in Sartre's short story, *The Childhood of a Leader*, resorts to racism as a means of alleviating the anguish that the transcendence of the Other inspires in him. He negates the freedom of the Other and the threat it presents by considering the Other to be a thing, a type, a stereotype. Lucien convinces himself that the foreigners around him have an existence less substantial and significant than his own. He considers their behaviour to be a caused phenomenon rather than the direct expression of their freedom, and in so doing reduces them to a facticity. Sartre writes:

> All the dagos were floating in dark, heavy waters whose eddies jolted their flabby flesh, raised their arms, agitated their fingers and played a little with their lips . . . They could dress in clothes from the Boulevard Saint-Michel in vain; they were hardly more than jellyfish. Lucien thought, he was not a jellyfish, he did not belong to that humiliated race. (*CL*, pp. 215–16)

12 An example of the kind of individual Catalano refers to is US Colonel Oliver North. North is associated with the Iran–Contra affair of the 1980s. On 1 December 1986 North evoked the fifth amendment to avoid telling the truth about the affair. Later, however, he confessed with deep sincerity to a US joint congressional hearing (7–15 July 1987) his role in an administration that had contrived to deceive the American people. North's sincere confession about his deceit gave him such a reputation for honesty with many Americans that he was able to run for political office on the strength of it (*Keesing's Record of World Events* 1987, pp. 35182–7).

CHAPTER 6: THE FAITH OF BAD FAITH: THE PRIMITIVE PROJECT

1 Fingarette's distinction between a mode of consciousness in which we spell out what we are doing and a mode of consciousness in which we do not spell out what we are doing is very similar to Sartre's distinction between reflective and pre-reflective consciousness.
2 When we do spell out what we are doing, particularly in the form of reflecting upon what we are doing as we do it, we tend to lose concentration and fail to do the job well. Some people, for example, fail to drive well when they have passengers in their car because they are distracted by the thought of how their performance appears to their passengers. This is as true for some confident drivers as it is for nervous drivers. Distracted by the thought of how impressive their driving appears to their passengers, some confident (over-confident?) drivers will fail to give full attention to the task in hand. One reason why 'Pride goeth before destruction' (Proverbs 16.18).
3 Increasing the number of believers in a particular religious doctrine, for example, does not make the doctrine any the less uncertain. Evangelism, the drive to recruit believers to a doctrine, is a reaction to the uncertainty inherent in religious faith. An evangelist concerns himself with the belief

of others in order to distract himself from the fact that his own belief is just a belief. If he confronted his own belief he would expose it as necessarily uncertain, so he preoccupies himself with the belief of others. For him, the belief of others is belief-in-itself, an object-belief firmly founded upon itself rather than a mere disposition founded upon a fragile suspension of disbelief. He is in bad faith towards others because he denies them their freedom by regarding them as believer-things incapable of transcending their 'state of conviction'. (If any of them ceased to believe he would regard them as corrupted or deluded, not as having reached a decision of their own free will.) In this respect he is the same as Sartre's champion of sincerity who wants his homosexual friend to accept the label 'homosexual' (*BN*, pp. 63–4). An evangelist champions sincerity regarding belief with the aim of reducing others to receptacles of belief-in-itself. Belief is thereby transformed into a public object that the evangelist can then take possession of. Unable to believe without doubt in his own belief he partakes in the supposedly certain belief-in-itself of others by regarding himself as simply another other. Recall that the primitive project of bad faith allows a person to see himself exclusively from the point of view of others. Religious faith often involves a person objectifying his own faith through the objectification of the faith of others.

CHAPTER 7:   SARTRE ON AUTHENTICITY

1 Ronald Santoni writes:

> we can see, by following some of Sartre's remarks and contentions in *The War Diaries*, that his view of authenticity here relates centrally to his view of the 'human condition', to his phenomenological ontology, to his account of the human project and the way in which human reality faces its 'condition'. (Santoni 1995, p. 90)

2 The only choice that is an escape from choice is the choice to commit suicide. Arguably, suicide is not an affirmation of freedom but an absolute denial of freedom achieved through the final annihilation of the for-itself. Arguably, suicide is an act of bad faith; 'the coward's way out', as the saying goes. The problem with this view is that committing suicide seems to be a far from cowardly act in that it involves overcoming the deepest fears – fear of no turning back, fear of final agony, fear of the unknown.

3 Nietzsche identifies 'the *narrowing of perspective*, and thus in a certain sense stupidity, as a condition of life and growth' (Nietzsche 1990, 188, p. 112). As they say in Yorkshire, it is wise to be 'thick ont' right side'.

4 The expert in existentialism referred to is Martin Heidegger. Heidegger was certainly a member of Hitler's National Socialist Party, but to what extent he agreed with its ideology and how much he knew of its barbarity is less certain. In his book *Heidegger*, George Steiner writes, 'Like millions of other German men and women, and a good many eminent minds outside Germany, Heidegger was caught up in the electric trance of the National Socialist promise' (Steiner 1992, p. 121). His enthusiasm,

however, did not last long, and he left the party in 1934 after being a member for only nine months. Nonetheless, Steiner continues, 'The spate of articles and speeches of 1933–34 cries out against Martin Heidegger. For here he goes so crassly beyond official obligation, let alone a provisional endorsement' (Steiner 1992, p. 121). Steiner concludes that Heidegger's real culpability lies in the fact that he never took the opportunity to retract the opinions expressed in these articles and speeches after the Second World War. 'Nauseating as they are, Heidegger's gestures and pronouncements during 1933–34 are tractable. It is his complete silence on Hitlerism and the Holocaust after 1945 which is very nearly intolerable' (Steiner 1992, p. 123).

5 Plato, in *The Republic*, likens the process of enlightenment to the passage of a person from a world of shadows within a cave out into the clear light of day (Plato 2003, Book 6, 514a–21b).

CHAPTER 8:   SARTRE AND NIETZSCHE

1 For Sartre, positive and negative freedom constitute what Maurice Natanson refers to as 'two fundamental modes of choice'. He writes: 'Either the self chooses self-consciously, wills its actions positively; or it seeks to flee from the grave responsibility of having to make choices' (*Natanson* 1962, p. 67).

2 Jacob Golomb writes: 'The will to power is of a piece with the quest for authenticity – the will to become a free author (within the necessary limits) of one's own self. The optimal will to power is expressed by the ideally authentic Übermensch' (Golomb 1990, p. 254).

3 Catalano's use of 'good faith' here equates to 'authenticity' rather than to 'sincerity'.

CHAPTER 9:   SARTRE AND HEIDEGGER

1 'Ownmost': most its own (from the German '*eigenst*').

2 In Christopher Marlowe's account, Doctor Faustus sells his soul to Lucifer in exchange for 24 years of wealth and power. The time inevitably runs out until Faustus knows he has only one hour of life remaining before Lucifer claims him. 'Ah, Faustus, / Now hast thou but one bare hour to live' (Marlowe 2003, V, ii).

REFERENCES

Allison, Henry E., 1983, *Kant's Transcendental Idealism: An Interpretation and Defence* (London: Yale University Press).

Anselm, 1965, *Proslogion*, trans. M.J. Charlesworth (Oxford: Clarendon Press).

Berkeley, George, 1988, *Principles of Human Knowledge* (Harmondsworth: Penguin).

Brentano, Franz, 1973, *Psychology from an Empirical Standpoint*, trans. A. Rancurello and D. Terrell (London: Routledge & Kegan Paul).

Catalano, Joseph, 1993, 'Good and bad faith: weak and strong notions', in Keith Hoeller (ed.), *Sartre and Psychology* (Atlantic Highlands, NJ: Humanities Press International).

Compton, John J., 1982, 'Sartre, Merleau-Ponty and human freedom', *Journal of Philosophy* 79: 577–88.

Cooper, David E., 1996, *Heidegger* (London: Claridge Press).

de Beauvoir, Simone, 1955, 'Merleau-Ponty et le pseudo-Sartrisme', *Les Temps modernes* 10: 2072–122.

——, 2000, *The Ethics of Ambiguity*, trans. Bernard Frechtman (New York: Citadel Press).

Demos, Raphael, 1960, 'Lying to oneself', *Journal of Philosophy* 57: 588–95.

Descartes, René, 1983, *Meditations on First Philosophy*, in Margaret D. Wilson (ed.), *The Essential Descartes* (New York: Meridian).

Dostoevsky, Fyodor, 1951, *Crime and Punishment*, trans. David Magarshack (Harmondsworth: Penguin).

——, 1958, *The Brothers Karamazov*, trans. David Magarshack (Harmondsworth: Penguin).

Fell, Joseph P., 1983, *Heidegger and Sartre: An Essay on Being and Place* (New York: Columbia University Press).

Fingarette, Herbert, 2000, *Self-Deception* (Berkeley, CA: University of California Press).

Freud, Sigmund, 1986, 'The Ego and the Id', in Freud, *The Essentials of Psychoanalysis*, trans. James Strachey (Harmondsworth: Penguin).

Golomb, Jacob, 1990, 'Nietzsche on authenticity', *Philosophy Today* 34: 243–58.

Greene, Norman N., 1980, *Jean-Paul Sartre: The Existentialist Ethic* (Oxford: Greenwood Press).

Grene, Marjorie, 1983, *Sartre* (Lanham, MD: University Press of America).

Hegel, George Wilhelm Friedrich, 1998, *Science of Logic*, trans. A.V. Miller (New York: Prometheus).

——, 2003, *The Phenomenology of Mind*, trans. J.B. Bailey (New York: Dover).

Heidegger, Martin, 1978, 'What is metaphysics?', in David Farrell Krell (ed.), *Heidegger: Basic Writings* (London: Routledge & Kegan Paul).

——, 1993, *Being and Time*, trans. John Macquarrie and Edward Robinson (Oxford: Blackwell).

Husserl, Edmund, 1977, *Cartesian Meditations: An Introduction to Phenomenology*, trans. Dorion Cairns (The Hague: Martinus Nijhoff).

Johnson, Samuel, 1952, 'Letter to Mrs Thrale – Wed. 17 March 1773', in R.W. Chapman (ed.), *Letters of Samuel Johnson*, Vol.1 (Oxford: Oxford University Press).

Kamber, Richard, 2000, *On Sartre* (Belmont, CA: Wadsworth).

Kant, Immanuel, 1990, *Critique of Pure Reason*, trans. Norman Kemp Smith (London: Macmillan).

Keesing's Record of World Events Vol. 33, 1987, Roger East (ed.) (Harlow: Longman).

Kierkegaard, Søren, 1989, *The Sickness unto Death: A Christian Psychological Exposition for Edification and Awakening*, trans. Alastair Hannay (Harmondsworth: Penguin).

Laing, R.D., 1990, *The Divided Self: An Existential Study in Sanity and Madness* (Harmondsworth: Penguin).

Langer, Monika, 1981, 'Sartre and Merleau-Ponty: a reappraisal', in Paul Schilpp (ed.), *The Philosophy of Jean-Paul Sartre*, Library of Living Philosophers Vol. 16 (La Salle, IL: Open Court).

Leibniz, Gottfried Wilhelm, 1990a, *Monadology*, in G.H.R. Parkinson (ed.), *Leibniz, Philosophical Writings* (London: Everyman/J.M. Dent).

——, 1990b, *On Freedom*, in G.H.R. Parkinson (ed.), *Leibniz, Philosophical Writings* (London: Everyman/J.M. Dent).

Manser, Anthony, 1981, *Sartre: A Philosophic Study* (Oxford: Greenwood Press).

——, 1987, 'A new look at bad faith', in Simon Glynn (ed.), *Sartre: An Investigation of Some Major Themes* (Aldershot: Avebury).

Marlowe, Christopher, 2003, *The Tragical History of the Life and Death of Doctor Faustus*, (ed.), Roma Gill (London: A & C Black).

McCulloch, Gregory, 1994, *Using Sartre: An Analytical Introduction to Early Sartrean Themes* (London: Routledge).

McGill, V.J., 1949, 'Sartre's doctrine of freedom', *Revue internationale de philosophie 2*.

Merleau-Ponty, Maurice, 2002, *Phenomenology of Perception*, trans. Colin Smith (London: Routledge).

Midgley, Mary, 2002, *Beast and Man: The Roots of Human Nature* (London: Routledge).

Natanson, Maurice, 1962, 'Sartre's philosophy of freedom', in Natanson,

Literature, Philosophy and the Social Sciences (The Hague: Martinus Nijhoff).

Nietzsche, Friedrich, 1974, *The Gay Science*, trans. Walter Kaufmann (New York: Vintage Press).

——, 1979, *Ecce Homo*, trans. R.J. Hollingdale (Harmondsworth: Penguin).

——, 1988, *Thus Spoke Zarathustra*, trans. R.J. Hollingdale (Harmondsworth: Penguin).

——, 1990a, *Beyond Good and Evil: Prelude to a Philosophy of the Future*, trans. R.J. Hollingdale (Harmondsworth: Penguin).

——, 1990b, *The Genealogy of Morals*, trans. Francis Golffing (New York: Anchor/Doubleday).

Plato, 1960, *Gorgias*, trans. Walter Hamilton (Harmondsworth: Penguin).

——, 2003, *The Republic*, trans. Desmond Lee (Harmondsworth: Penguin).

Robbins, C.W., 1977, 'Sartre and the moral life', *Philosophy* 12: 409–24.

Ryle, Gilbert, 1990, *The Concept of Mind* (Harmondsworth: Penguin).

Santoni, Ronald E., 1995, *Bad Faith, Good Faith and Authenticity in Sartre's Early Philosophy* (Philadelphia, PA: Temple University Press).

Sartre, Jean-Paul, 1960, *The Childhood of a Leader*, in Sartre, *Intimacy*, trans. Lloyd Alexander (London: Panther Books).

——, 1964, *The Problem of Method*, trans. Hazel E. Barnes (London: Methuen).

——, 1964, *Saint Genet*, trans. Bernard Frechtmann (New York: Mentor).

——, 1974, *Anti-Semite and Jew*, trans. George J. Becker (New York: Schocken).

——, 1983, *Lettres au Castor* (Paris: Gallimard).

——, 1986, *The Age of Reason*, trans. David Caute (Harmondsworth: Penguin).

——, 1986, *Being and Nothingness*, trans. Hazel E. Barnes (London: Methuen).

——, 1987, *Nausea*, trans. Robert Baldick (Harmondsworth: Penguin).

——, 1989, *No Exit and Three Other Plays* (New York: Vintage).

——, 1991, *Words*, trans. Irene Clephane (Harmondsworth: Penguin).

——, 1993, *Existentialism and Humanism*, trans. Philip Mairet (London: Methuen).

——, 1994, *The Transcendence of the Ego: An Existentialist Theory of Consciousness*, trans. Forrest Williams and Robert Kirkpartrick (New York: Hill & Wang).

——, 1995, *Crime Passionnel (Les mains sales)*, trans. Kitty Black (London: Methuen).

——, 1999, *War Diaries: Notebooks from a Phoney War, 1939–1940*, trans. Q. Hoare (London: Verso).

Spinoza, Benedictus de, 1992, *Ethics*, trans. Andrew Boyle and G.H.R. Parkinson (London: Everyman/J.M. Dent).

Steiner, George, 1992, *Heidegger* (London: HarperCollins/Fontana).

Wider, Kathleen V., 1997, *The Bodily Nature of Consciousness: Sartre and Contemporary Philosophy of Mind* (Ithaca, NY: Cornell University Press).

REFERENCES

Wittgenstein, Ludwig, 1980, *Remarks on the Philosophy of Psychology*, trans. G.G. Luckhardt and M.A.E. Ave (Oxford: Basil Blackwell).
——, 1988, *Philosophical Investigations*, trans. G.E.M. Anscombe (Oxford: Basil Blackwell).
——, 2001, *Tractatus Logico-Philosophicus*, trans. D.F. Pears and B.F. McGuiness (London: Routledge).

FURTHER READING

Barnes, Hazel E., *Sartre* (London: Quartet Books, 1974).

Danto, Arthur C., *Sartre* (London: HarperCollins/Fontana, 1991).

Detmer, David, *Freedom as a Value: A Critique of the Ethical Theory of Jean-Paul Sartre* (La Salle, IL: Open Court, 1986).

Hammond, Michael, Jane Howarth and Russell Keat, *Understanding Phenomenology* (Oxford: Blackwell, 1992).

Howells, Christina (ed.), *The Cambridge Companion to Sartre* (Cambridge: Cambridge University Press, 1992).

King, Magda, *Heidegger's Philosophy; A Guide to his Basic Thought* (Oxford: Basil Blackwell, 1964).

Levy, Neil, *Sartre* (Oxford: Oneworld, 2002).

McBride, William L. (ed.), *Sartre and Existentialism: Philosophy, Politics, Ethics, The Psyche, Literature and Aesthetics, Volumes 1–8* (London: Garland/Taylor & Francis, 1997).

Murdoch, Iris, *Sartre: Romantic Rationalist* (London: Vintage, 1999).

Myerson, George, *Sartre: A Beginner's Guide* (London: Hodder & Stoughton, 2001).

Natanson, Maurice, *A Critique of Jean-Paul Sartre's Ontology* (Lincoln, NB: University of Nebraska Press, 1951).

Nehamas, Alexander, *Nietzsche: Life as Literature* (Cambridge, MA: Harvard University Press, 1985).

Priest, Stephen (ed.), *Jean-Paul Sartre: Basic Writings* (London and New York: Routledge, 2001).

Sartre, Jean-Paul, *Sketch for a Theory of the Emotions*, trans. Philip Mairet (London: Methuen, 1985).

Stathern, Paul, *The Essential Sartre* (London: Virgin Books, 2002).

Warnock, Mary, *Existentialism* (Oxford: Oxford University Press, 1970).

INDEX

absurdity 157n
absence *see* existential absence *and*
  formal absence
action 52, 62, 66, 68, 73, 78–80, 85,
  97–8, 100, 106, 113, 125, 146,
  163n
actor 101–3
addiction 30
afterlife 54, 154
Allison, Henry 158–9n
ambition 105–6
anger 56, 107
anguish 46, 100, 106, 124–6, 129, 143,
  166n
annihilation 33, 98, 103, 154–5, 167n
Anselm 8–9, 158n
anxiety *see* anguish
appearances 13–15, 17, 20–2
ascetic ideal 146
atheism 54
authenticity 120, 129, 133, 135–48,
  150–3, 167n, 168n
autonomy 80

bad faith 9, 40, 45, 84, 91–9, 101–3,
  105, 109, 113–21, 123–7, 129,
  133–5, 138–40, 142–3, 145–50,
  152, 164–5n, 165n, 166–7n, 167n
  faith of bad faith 123
becoming 5, 36–7, 98, 106, 122, 157n
being 3–6, 157n; *see also* being-in-itself
  undifferentiated being 4, 15, 21–6,
  31, 36, 52
being-for-itself 7–12, 21–3, 26–7, 32–7,
  39, 40–2, 44, 49–54, 61, 64–8,
  71–2, 75, 79–80, 91, 96, 99, 101,

106–7, 114, 121–2, 135, 138–9,
  155, 161–2n, 167n
being for itself-in-itself 8–9, 27, 35,
  41, 68, 98, 108, 135, 138, 142,
  161–2n
being-for-others 42, 44–7, 49
being-in-itself 6–9, 11, 15, 21, 23–5,
  35, 64–5, 67, 102
being-in-situation 136–7, 142, 144
being-in-the-midst-of-the-world 44,
  48–9, 96
being-in-the-world 44, 48, 50, 54, 96
belief 128, 149, 166–7n
Berkeley, George 15–17, 158n
body 42, 49–56, 81–2, 96–9, 161n; *see
  also* embodiment
Bourget, Paul 161–2n
brain 18–20, 108
Brentano, Franz 13

Catalano, Joseph 119, 149–50, 166n,
  168n
category mistake 108, 165n
causal order 62, 64
censorship 94–5
chastity 146
choice 62, 65, 68–83, 85–7, 91, 98,
  111–13, 126, 134–6, 139, 167n,
  168n
  fundamental choice 9, 68–9, 161–2n
  groundless choice 85–6, 161–2n
  negative choice 98
  positive choice 98
  radical choice 85
Christianity 120, 164–5n
closed circuit television camera 160n

cognitive science 20
commitment 72, 126–7, 144
compatibilism 62, 109
Compton, John 81, 112
confession 114, 118–20, 126
conflict 46–7
consciousness 4, 7, 10–12, 14–15,
  17–18, 20–6, 29, 31, 36–43, 49, 51,
  53–5, 61, 63, 66, 68, 76, 80, 82–3,
  91–5, 97, 109–11, 113, 141, 160n,
  163n, 163–4n, 164n, 166n
  buffeted consciousness 136–7, 140
  class consciousness 77
  disembodied consciousness 54
  false consciousness 123, 149
  non-thetic consciousness 38–9, 55
  non-thetic self-consciousness 37–8,
    160n
  positional consciousness 37–8
  pre-reflective consciousness 37–9,
    164n, 166n
  reflected-on consciousness 39–41
  reflective consciousness 38–41,
    164n, 166n
  self-consciousness 37–41, 55, 56,
    103, 124, 161–2n
  thetic consciousness 38–9, 160n
  thetic self-consciousness 37–9
Cooper, David 152
Copernican Revolution 24
coping strategy 126, 143
cowardice 69–70, 121, 143

Dasein 32–3, 36, 151
de Beauvoir, Simone 66, 68, 102–3,
  114, 153, 163n
death 70, 106, 143, 151–5, 167n,
  168n
  being-towards-death 106, 151–5
deception 92–3
  self-deception 92–5, 97, 114
Demos, Raphael 93–4
depression 111
Descartes, René 15–17, 63–4, 158n
desire 26–8, 94–5, 112, 161–2n
despair 110–11
destruction 31
determination 73
determinism 61–4, 66, 163n
disability 76, 83–4
disappointment 28
distraction 97

Dostoevsky, Fyodor 119, 120, 126,
  148
double property 95–6, 99, 117
doubt 128

ego 41, 94–5
ekstasis 33, 160n
embodiment 54–6, 97, 99
emotional states 55, 111, 113
enlightenment 143
enslavement 45
escape 66, 101, 109, 111, 116–19, 122,
  135, 164–5n, 167n
esse est percipi 16; see also idealism
eternal recurrence 148
evangelism 166–7n
evasion 97
everydayness 153
evil 108, 118–19, 147
excuses 137, 141
existential absence 26, 29, 30, 71
existential project 77–8
existential psychoanalysis 161–2n
existential truths 78, 127, 142–3
existentialism 54, 74, 76, 87, 133, 135,
  140, 143, 157n, 161n, 167–8n
existentialist ethics 87
existentialist ideal 140, 142
expectation 29–30
external relation 64, 93, 163n

facticity 65–6, 68, 85, 96, 98–9, 101,
  106, 108, 113, 115–17, 122, 125,
  134–6, 139, 145, 163–4n
faith 127–8, 149, 150, 166–7n
fatigue 83–4
fear 111, 124, 126, 153, 167n
Fell, Joseph 160n
figure-ground 22–3, 159n
Fingarette, Herbert 93–4, 127–8, 166n
Flaubert, Gustave 161–2n
flight 33–5, 40, 66, 68, 96–8, 138–9,
  164–5n
flirt 92, 96–9, 116–17, 134
forgiveness 120
for-itself see being-for-itself
for-itself-in-itself see being-for-itself-
  in-itself
formal absence 29, 71
Forms 31, 159–60n
formula for greatness 148
free will 61–4, 66, 163n

freedom 10, 45, 61–8, 70–85, 87, 91–2, 101, 109, 111, 116–18, 125–6, 135–6, 138–9, 142–4, 146–8, 155, 163n, 166n
  affirmation of freedom 135–6, 138–9, 146, 148, 150–3, 167n
  assumption of freedom 136, 139–40, 143, 151
  negative freedom 146–7, 168n
  positive freedom 147, 168n
Freud, Sigmund 93–5, 164n
fundamental project 161–2n
future 9, 32–5, 37, 51–2, 54, 64–70, 74, 75, 78, 96–7, 106, 115, 119, 151
future-past 33–4, 66
futurising intention 37

genius 106
Gestalt School 159n
God 8–9, 16, 21, 43, 63, 68, 120, 128, 158n, 160n, 161–2n
Golomb, Jacob 168n
good faith 102, 114, 116–17, 120, 149, 150, 168n
Greene, Norman 161n
Grene, Marjorie 47
guilt 46, 114, 117–18, 120, 126

Hamlet 101–2, 104–5
hand 52–4, 96–7
happiness 72
Hegel, George Wilhelm Friedrich 4–7, 12, 21, 24, 64, 157n, 158n
Heidegger, Martin 32–3, 36, 44, 47, 50, 52–3, 106, 151–3, 155, 159n, 160n, 167–8n
Heraclitus 5
heroic ideal 140, 144
homosexual 114–17, 134, 165n
homosexuality 84, 121
homunculus problem 19–20
horizons 14
human condition 61, 74, 140, 142–3, 151, 167n
human nature 74
humour see sense of humour
Husserl, Edmund 13, 14
hypnosis 84, 163n
hysteria 107–8

Id 94
idealism 15, 158n

ignorance 93, 143
immortality 106
impersonation 103–4
inaction 79
inauthenticity 134–6, 138–9, 141–5, 147
in-itself see being-in-itself
inner observer 19, 20
insanity 82, 84, 104, 108, 113, 127, 149
insincerity 103, 114, 117, 147
instinct 94, 125
instrumentality 52–3
intellectual project 76–8, 82, 142–3
intention 26, 68, 73
intentional object 13, 17, 37–9, 41, 110
intentionality 12–13, 20
internal relation 64, 163–4n
Iran-Contra Affair 166n
irony 103

jealousy 55
Johnson, Samuel 111

Kamber, Richard 9
Kant, Immanuel 21, 158n
Kierkegaard, Søren 110–11, 124
knowledge 11, 18, 39, 95, 97, 164n

lack 26–7, 30, 36, 67, 70–2, 79, 106, 159n, 161–2n
Laing R.D. 108, 157n, 161–2n
Langer, Monika 163n
Leibniz, Gottfried Wilhelm 63, 158n
look 44–6
love 27, 30, 72, 109, 112, 141, 144

madness see insanity
make-believe 102–3, 149
Manser, Anthony 86, 115, 161n, 165n
Marlowe, Christopher 168n
masochism 46, 160n
master 164–5n
McCulloch, Gregory 15–16, 47, 82, 84–5
McGill, V.J. 82–4, 86–7, 163n
Merleau-Ponty, Maurice 56, 76–82, 85, 87, 112, 163n
metastable 96, 139, 164n
Midgley, Mary 157n
Mitsein 47
moral agency 86–7
moral dilemma 86

moral values 86–7
morality 86–7
  private morality 86
mortality 152–4
  affirmation of mortality 151–3
motion 23–4, 32
motives 70, 153, 165n

Natanson, Maurice 168n
natural self 81–2, 85, 87, 112
negation 4–9, 12, 21–3, 25–7, 29–30,
  33, 35, 39–40, 51, 64–6, 98, 155,
  160n
  concrete negation 21–2
  double negation 9, 21
  internal negation 45, 64
  original negation 36, 62
  radical negation 21–2
négatités see negativities
negativities (négatités) 22, 70, 155
neurosis 84, 126
Nietzsche, Friedrich 46, 126, 138,
  146–8, 164–5n, 167n
nihilation 40, 51, 158n
nihilism 102–3, 138, 149–50
  faith of nihilism 149
nobility 140–1
noble ideal 146–7
non-being 3–9, 21, 26–7, 29, 31, 33, 68,
  157n; see also nothingness
non-being-in-itself 8, 102–3, 115, 138,
  149
not noticing 93–4
not spelling-out 127–8, 166n
nothingness 3, 5–8, 24, 27, 31, 65–6,
  101–2, 155, 157n, 160n, 164–5n;
  see also non-being
nothingness-in-itself 102
noumenon (thing-in-itself) 13–14, 21,
  158–9n

Ontological Argument 8–9, 158n
ontological level 8, 10, 12
ontology 5, 25, 32, 63, 167n
opacity 37–8, 95
original synthesis 62, 115
other minds 47–8, 161n
other people 42–6, 48–9, 54–7, 92–3,
  100, 106, 154
overcoming 71, 79, 106, 129, 140,
  146
overman see Ubermensch

panic 82–3, 113
Parmenides 159n
past 9, 32–5, 37, 51–2, 64, 66, 69–70,
  82, 98, 115, 119, 121, 134, 141,
  148, 163n
past-future 33–4, 66
perfect moments 28
performance 100, 102–4, 127, 137,
  149–50
persistent vegetative state 80, 163n
personality 80, 106, 161–2n
phenomenalism 15
phenomenological level 8, 12
phenomenology 10, 13–14, 26, 32, 36,
  61–3, 92, 154
phobias 125–6
Picture Gallery Model of the Mind
  16–20
Plato 143, 159n, 159–60n, 168n
playing 100–14, 107, 165n
presence 30, 35, 64
  co-presence 35
present 33–5, 37, 52, 64, 66, 151
present-at-hand 53
pre-structure 81, 82, 87, 112
pretence 102–3, 137, 165n
primitive project 123–4, 127–9, 149,
  166–7n
private language 86
pseudo-irreducibles 161–2n
psyche 41, 163n
psychic duality 95
psychic objects 41, 118, 160n
psychoanalysis see existential
  psychoanalysis
psychology 10, 18–19, 61, 107–8, 159n
psychosis 84, 127
Pythagoras 159n

quasi-duality 164n
questioning attitude 22

radical conversion 120, 133, 136, 147,
  153
Raskolnikov 120–1, 126, 148
ready-to-hand 53
realism 15, 20–1, 24–5, 36–7
rebirth 120–1
reductionism 10, 20
regret 137–9, 142, 147–8, 150, 152
reinvention 112
religious doctrine 166–7n

representation 67, 101
repression 94–5, 146
responsibility 62, 76, 80, 84–5, 97, 99,
    108, 113, 118, 134–6, 138–9, 141,
    143–4, 146, 148, 152, 163n
    diminished responsibility 84
resurrection 120
revolution 77–8
Robbins, C. W. 86
Ryle, Gilbert 108, 165n

sadness 106–12
Santoni, Ronald 139, 167n
satisfaction 27–8, 143
schizophrenia 108
Schopenhauer, Arthur 46
self-denial 79, 146
self-reflection 103
self-respect 140
sensations 18–19
sense of humour 82–3
sexual arousal 160n
sexual preference 82, 84–5
sexual relationships 160n
Shakespeare, William 102, 104–5,
    107–8, 153
shame 42, 46, 55, 160n
sincerity 103, 105, 113–14, 116–19,
    121–2, 126, 134–5, 147, 166n,
    166–7n, 168n
    champion of sincerity 114–17,
    134–5, 166–7n
situatedness 26, 32, 51, 72, 75, 98–9,
    136–7, 144
slave ethic 164–5n
sleep 95, 124
smoking 70–2
social conformity 144
solipsism 16, 158n
spelling-out 127–8, 166n
Steiner, George 167–8n
stereotyping 10, 114, 116, 166n
stupidity 144, 167n
success 106, 126

suicide 152, 167n
surpassing 6, 27, 32, 34, 44, 51, 64–6,
    74,
suspension of disbelief 102, 127,
    166–7

temporality 9, 32–7, 40, 51, 64
thing-in-itself see noumenon
tongue in cheek 103
Tourette's syndrome 108
transcendence 41, 44–6, 50–1, 54, 62,
    64–6, 70, 96–100, 105–6, 110,
    114–18, 121–2, 125, 134–5, 145
transcendence transcended 44–6, 56,
    99–101, 160n
transcendence-in-itself 98
transcendent object 41
transcendent subject 44–5
transcendental idealism 15, 20–1,
    23–5, 31, 36
translucency 38, 92, 110
transparency 80, 95
transphenomenality 14
twins 75

Ubermensch (overman) 147, 149–50,
    153, 168n
unconscious 93–5, 164n
upsurge 11
useless passion 28–9, 110, 161–2n

vertigo 124–5
visual field 50
voyeurism 45

waiter 92, 100–1, 103–5, 107, 109, 127,
    137, 149, 165n
Warnock, Mary 191n
Wider, Kathleen 55–6
will to power 146–7, 168n
Wittgenstein, Ludwig 50, 86, 128, 154,
    161n

Zeno's paradoxes 23, 159n